Cambridge Elements

Elements in the History of Constantinople
edited by
Peter Frankopan
University of Oxford

THE CHORA MONASTERY OF CONSTANTINOPLE

Emmanuel S. Moutafov
Bulgarian Academy of Sciences

Shaftesbury Road, Cambridge CB2 8EA, United Kingdom

One Liberty Plaza, 20th Floor, New York, NY 10006, USA

477 Williamstown Road, Port Melbourne, VIC 3207, Australia

314–321, 3rd Floor, Plot 3, Splendor Forum, Jasola District Centre,
New Delhi – 110025, India

103 Penang Road, #05–06/07, Visioncrest Commercial, Singapore 238467

Cambridge University Press is part of Cambridge University Press & Assessment,
a department of the University of Cambridge.

We share the University's mission to contribute to society through the pursuit of education, learning and research at the highest international levels of excellence.

www.cambridge.org
Information on this title: www.cambridge.org/9781009486804

DOI: 10.1017/9781108946476

When citing this work, please include a reference to the DOI 10.1017/9781108946476

First published 2024

A catalogue record for this publication is available from the British Library

ISBN 978-1-009-48680-4 Hardback
ISBN 978-1-108-93113-7 Paperback
ISSN 2514-3891 (online)
ISSN 2514-3883 (print)

The Chora Monastery of Constantinople

Elements in the History of Constantinople

DOI: 10.1017/9781108946476
First published online: December 2024

Emmanuel S. Moutafov
Bulgarian Academy of Sciences

Author for correspondence: Emmanuel S. Moutafov, moutafov1@gmail.com

Abstract: The Chora is one of the most celebrated churches built in Constantinople during the Byzantine era (330–1453). It is particularly famous for its glorious mosaics and frescoes, mostly dating to the fourteenth century, which are a particularly fine example of Late Byzantine art. After the Ottoman conquest of Constantinople in 1453, the church was repurposed as a mosque, known as the Kariye Camii. Between 1945 and 2020, it had another incarnation, as the Kariye Museum, but then in 2020, in line with changing Turkish governmental policies, it again became a mosque. This Element sets out the history of the building, presents its artwork, and considers how best to interpret its construction, significance, and meaning. Above all, it offers an insight into images and words that are currently inaccessible to the general public.

Keywords: Chora, Byzantine art, Palaiologan art, Constantinople, Byzantine epigraphy

ISBNs: 9781009486804 (HB), 9781108931137 (PB), 9781108946476 (OC)
ISSNs: 2514-3891 (online), 2514-3883 (print)

Contents

Introduction

Constructed in the late eleventh century, the Church of the Chora – the *katholikon* (main church) of the Chora monastery – is one of the best-known churches of the Byzantine era (c. 330–1453). Its mosaics and frescoes, created during the Palaiologan period (1261–1453, when the Palaiologoi were the ruling dynasty), are some of the most sumptuous to have been commissioned in the imperial capital of Constantinople (modern Istanbul). The walls and the dome of the church are decorated with mosaics and frescoes of exceptional artistic quality, many of which depict scenes from the lives of Christ and the Theotokos (Mother of God, the Virgin Mary). The most well-known patron of the monastery, Theodore Metochites (c. 1270–1332), is famously depicted in the church, but other important portraits and memorials to be found there, which often receive less attention in scholarship, also contribute much to our understanding of the Byzantine period and its people.

After the Fall of Constantinople to the Ottomans in 1453, the church became a mosque, known as the Kariye Camii. It was decommissioned after the Second World War and turned into a museum in 1958, undergoing heavy restoration over the decades. Since 2020, when it was reconverted into a mosque, the mosaics and frescoes have not been accessible to the general public.

This Element discusses the Chora, drawing on and complementing the work of many other scholars. In doing so, it seeks to explain the history of the complex, to introduce and illustrate its magnificent mosaics and frescoes, and to put the building and its uses into historical context.[1]

History of the Monastery

Origins

Tradition has it that Constantinople, like Rome,[2] was built on seven hills; and it was on one of these hills that the Chora complex was built, to the south of the Golden Horn, in what is now the district of Edirnekapı.

The first Church of the Chora – which, like its later incarnation, was the *katholikon* of a monastery complex – was built on a site located outside the walls built by the Emperor Constantine (r. 312–337) when, in the early fourth century, he invested considerable resources in building a city to rival Rome. This older fifth-century church, likely built around a hundred years after the building of the Constantinian Walls, was named ‘en tè Chora’ – normally taken

[1] Moutafov, ‘Μονὴ Χώρας’; Moutafov, ‘On How’, pp. 199–212; Moutafov, *Богородица*.

[2] Underwood, ‘First Preliminary Report’, pp. 253–288, esp. 284–285; Ousterhout, *The Architecture*; Ousterhout, *The Art*, etc.

to mean 'in the countryside', to reflect its rural location relative to the main city, outside the Constantinian walls, even though by this time the church lay within the new set of walls built further out by the Emperor Theodosios II (r. 408–250). The later church retained the archaic reference to the countryside, and was formally known as the Church 'of the Holy Saviour in the Chora'. Today, it is usually simply referred to as 'the Chora'.

The name of the church has a further symbolic meaning, however: the two principal mosaics in the outer narthex bear inscriptions that refer to Christ as *Land of the Living* (*he Chora ton zonton*) and to Mary as *Container of the Uncontainable* (*he Chora tou Achoretou*), epithets that appear twice in the surviving iconographical programme – reflecting the church's identity as an intermediary space, linking together spiritual and physical worlds. The word *chora* used as an iconographical epithet refers mainly to the Theotokos, and derives from hymnography, although here it is apparently used for both Mary and Christ. This interpretation of the Chora is supported in the writings of the fourteenth-century patriarch Philotheos Kokkinos, who refers to it as '[t]hat humble monastic convent, which they have long called the Chora, whether the Land [Chora] of the Living – that is, of Christ – or the Container [Chora] of the Uncontainable Himself, I mean the Virgin and Mother of God'.[3]

History of the Church

The existence of the fifth-century church is known only from written sources, which give different accounts.[4] Some elements of the extant church have been considered to belong to the seventh century, because of archaic architectonic elements in the *naos* (nave) that are typical of Early Byzantine architecture – similar to churches like St Sophia in Thessaloniki and the Church of the Dormition in Nicaea, both built in this Early Byzantine period.[5]

However, recent research has shown that the church as it is known today has its origins in building work carried out between 1077 and 1081 under the patronage of Maria Doukaina, the mother-in-law of the Emperor Alexios I Komnenos (1081–1118).[6] This agrees with the Byzantine historian Nikephoras Gregoras' later attribution of the church to Maria, although

[3] τὸ σεπτὸν ἐκεῖνο τῶν μοναστῶν φροντιστήριον, ὃ Χώραν προσαγορεύουσιν ἄνωθεν, εἴτε τὴν τῶν ζώντων χώραν, δηλαδὴ τὸν Χριστόν, εἴτε τὴν τοῦ ἀχωρήτου χώραν αὐτοῦ τούτου, φημί, τὴν Παρθένον ἅμα καὶ Θεομήτορα (*Enc. Greg. Pal.* 133 Tsames). See Gennadios, 'Ὁ Πατριάρχης', p. 278. For details on the name of the church as an epithet of the Theotokos, see Moutafov 'Μονή Χώρας'; Moutafov, 'On How', pp. 199–212; Moutafov, *Богородица*, pp. 169–173.

[4] Underwood, 'First Preliminary Report', pp. 253–288, esp. 284–285.

[5] Gioles, *Βυζαντινή*, p. 94.

[6] Underwood, *The Kariye*; Ousterhout, *The Architecture*.

Komnenian sources do not mention the connection.[7] Maria's church was a cross-in-square with a small dome built upon four columns. This was the most common Byzantine church type from the ninth to fourteenth centuries.[8] Excavations in the 1950s discovered evidence of the narrow central apse and two lateral apses of Maria's church.

As a result of damage possibly caused by an earthquake, the building was then thoroughly remodelled c. 1120 by Maria's grandson, the *sebastokrator*[9] Isaak Komnenos (1093–c.1152). Isaak, son of Alexios I and brother of John II Komnenos, was a scholar and patron of distinction of churches both within the empire and in the Holy Land.[10]

During Isaak's reconstruction, the columns of Maria's church were replaced with corner supports (piers, πεσσοί) supporting broad arches and a larger dome. The nave was open eastward into a broad bema and apse, as one can see it today.[11] In the same period, John II, together with his wife Eirene/Piroska, was responsible for the construction of the Pantokrator monastery in Constantinople, the funeral chapel of which has a dome with a similar diameter to that of the Chora. The interior of the Chora *naos* was likely covered at this time with wall paintings rather than mosaics and marble, while the bema conch (altar niche) may have been decorated with mosaics, and the apse windows were filled with stained glass, like those of the Pantokrator, although they were produced separately.[12]

Isaak's connection to the Chora seems to have evolved over time. By the mid-twelfth century he was in exile in Thrace, where he founded the monastery of the Theotokos Kosmosoteira at Ferai (Vira), the *katholikon* of which survives, as does its Typikon of 1152.[13] This Typikon, a combination of a monastic charter and last will of the *sebastokrator* Isaak, shows that he had earlier had a tomb prepared for himself at the Chora, but then had it transferred to the Kosmosoteira.

In the first two decades of the fourteenth century, the Chora saw further significant changes, under the patronage of Theodore Metochites.[14] Metochites was one of the most eminent men in the empire in this period: a highly placed government official, diplomat, politician, philosopher, astronomer, historian, poet, theologian, and patron of the arts. As such, not only was he a powerful

[7] Gregoras, *Historia Byzantina*, IX.13.

[8] Ousterhout, *Finding a Place*, p. 19, where the author finds similarities between Maria's building and the church of Christ Pantepoptes (Eski Imaret Camii), rebuilt by Anna Dalassene, mother of Alexios I.

[9] Senior court title in the Late Byzantine empire, also used in the Byzantine sphere of influence; lit. in Greek 'venerable' + 'ruler'.

[10] Anderson, 'The Seraglio', pp. 83–114.

[11] This phase may be dated to the 1120s; see Ousterhout, *Finding a Place*, p. 23.

[12] Anderson, 'The Seraglio', p. 25.

[13] Ousterhout, *Finding a Place*, p. 23.

[14] *PLP*, no. 17982.

political figure but also one of the most prominent figures of the intellectual and artistic movement known as the 'Palaiologan Renaissance'. He was described by Nikephoras Gregoras as a 'living library' for his literary output; he also founded a library at the Chora.[15] He advanced in his career rapidly, becoming *mesazon* (sometimes compared to the role of 'prime minister') aged thirty-six, and eventually *megas logothetes* (Grand Logothete, supervisor of the state treasury), second only to the emperor himself. His daughter married into the imperial family.

With regard to his connection with the Chora, Metochites was appointed *ktetor* (owner, benefactor) of the monastery by Andronikos II;[16] the first non-imperial *ktetor* of a *basilike mone* (imperial monastery). He spent considerable sums adding to the Chora complex; his additions include the two narthexes and the *parekklesion* (south chapel), features characteristic of the tastes and fashions of Late Byzantine religious architecture. Because the Chora was built on unstable ground and had continued to shift downhill after the restorations of the early twelfth century, a flying buttress was also added, in an attempt to stabilise the altar apse.[17] Between 1315 and 1321,[18] or possibly slightly earlier,[19] Metochites endowed the monastery with its fine mosaics and frescoes. He planned to retire there.

When Andronikos III fell from power in 1328, Metochites' career also foundered, and he was banished to Didymoteichon in Thrace.[20] After two years, he was allowed to return to the capital, to be confined in the monastery he had rebuilt. He assumed the monastic name Theoleptos, which means 'containing God'. His most popular namesake, Theoleptos, Metropolitan of Philadelphia (1283/1284–1322), was an Orthodox theologian regarded by Gregory Palamas[21] as a forerunner of the mystical doctrine of hesychasm;[22] theologically, Metochites may have been influenced by these ideas. It is difficult to know whether Metochites retained his influence as patron and quasi-owner of the monastery when he returned to the Chora in 1330, ill and ousted from office. His burial place is not definitely known and, as will be seen, continues to attract speculation.

An Ottoman document discovered recently in the archives of the Vatopedi monastery gives some insight into the fortunes of the Chora in the century after

[15] A. Semoglou places Metochites' library at the Chora on the upper floor, in the south-west corner, where the minaret now rises: see Semoglou, 'L'éloquence', pp. 59–60.

[16] Ousterhout, *Finding a Place*, p. 14.

[17] Ousterhout, *The Architecture*, pp. 132–133.

[18] Ousterhout, *The Art*, p. 12.

[19] Smyrlis, 'Contextualizing', pp. 69–111. Smyrlis argues that Theodore Metochites became Grand Logothete between 1313/1314 and April 1317, which redates the period of his renovations at the Chora.

[20] Ševčenko, 'Theodore Metochites', p. 36.

[21] *PLP*, no. 21546.

[22] Talbot, 'Theoleptos', pp. 2056–2057.

Metochites' death. This document records that Mara Branković (daughter of George Branković and wife of Murad II) purchased the monastery shortly before passing away in 1487.[23] In that year, she gifted the Chora to the monastery of Vatopedi on Mt Athos as a *metochion* (dependent monastery); evidently, she had been patron and owner of the Chora. The text mentions an enclosure, and inside it, an oblong building and twenty-four monastic cells; outside the enclosure, a windmill with an oven and a storehouse, as well as vineyards nearby.[24]

Almost half a century after Constantinople fell to the Ottomans in 1453, Hadım Ali Pasha, Grand Vizier[25] to Sultan Bayezid II (1481–1512), ordered the building to be converted into a mosque, known first as the Ali Paşa Kenise Camii and later as the Kariye Camii. 'Kariye' means village/countryside in Arabic, and is a translation of the name Chora. The mosaics and frescoes were covered with a thick layer of plaster.

In the late nineteenth and early twentieth centuries, the Chora received attention from various quarters. In 1860, the Greek architect Pelopidas Kouppas recommended to the Sultan that restoration and renovation works should be carried out on the mosque. In 1903–1906, F. Shmit of the Russian Archaeological Institute in Constantinople led a programme of reinforcement works and research. In 1929, the Evkaf Administration (Administration of Foundations) was charged with the monument's conservation. In 1945, the Chora was designated a museum, the Kariye Müzesi, under the jurisdiction of the Ayasofya Museum. This redesignation was a continuation of the secularisation of the Turkish state instigated by Kemal Atatürk (c. 1881–1938). In 1948, the Byzantine Institute of America, in particular the Dumbarton Oaks Field Committee, undertook cleaning and conservation of the mosaics and murals and the building itself, and limited excavations. These works lasted throughout the 1950s, and in 1968, Paul A. Underwood published a three-volume study on the monument. Many further studies ensued, and the Church of the Chora became the most-published Byzantine monument. As has already been noted, the Church was again designated a mosque in August 2020.

[23] Kotzageorgis, 'Two Vakfiyes', pp. 307–322, esp. 221 and fig. 3. Mara Branković donated to the Rila monastery a miraculous icon of the Virgin Hodegetria with relics of thirty-two Constantinopolitan saints, some of them related to the Chora (Sts Floros and Lauros), which probably means that it was originally there before reaching Bulgaria in the fifteenth century; but this will be a subject of another publication.

[24] As described in Ousterhout, 'Introduction', p. 6.

[25] Title of the effective head of the government of many states in the Islamic world from the eighth century onwards. In the Ottoman Empire, the Grand Vizier held the imperial seal and was in charge of the other viziers, who were engaged with the affairs of the state mostly in administrative capacities.

The Fourteenth-Century Context: The Chora at Its Height

The art and architecture of the Chora as we know them today belong in the context of Byzantine revival after the vicissitudes of the thirteenth century, the period of the 'Latin Empire', when Constantinople fell to the Fourth Crusade and was under the rule of western Emperors from 1204 to 1261. Michael VIII, the founder of the Palaiologan dynasty, retook Constantinople in 1261, and the Palaiologan period that followed (1261–1453) saw a flourishing in many areas of cultural life, often referred to as the 'Palaiologan Renaissance'.

The conditions for artistic production in Constantinople between 1204 and 1261 are unclear, due to a lack of written records. Archaeological excavations also provide very little data. It is possible to discern a certain symbiosis of Byzantine and western elements in the capital, which bespeaks the existence of workshops capable of responding to the nationality and tastes of those commissioning artworks, whether Catholic or Orthodox.[26] However, during the Latin occupation, metalwork and stone were looted from the churches, and many Constantinopolitan relics, such as the Crown of Thorns, were sold outside Byzantine territories.[27] Gregoras paints a gloomy picture of the devastated city when the Byzantines returned: 'Enslaved, [Constantinople] had received no care from the Latins except destruction of every kind day and night. The first and most important immediate task facing the emperor was as much as possible to cleanse the city and transform its great disorder into good order, to strengthen the churches which had completely collapsed, and to fill the empty houses with people.'[28] This bleak account is probably no exaggeration,[29] although at the very least the Latin rulers did intervene to reinforce the walls of Hagia Sophia with new buttresses, perhaps after the earthquake of 1231.[30]

With the restoration of 1261, Constantinople quite naturally played a significant role in the ideology of the first Palaiologan emperor. In Palaiologan sources, the city was presented as 'the eye of Asia, the head of the Europe, a metropolis for the people in every land, wherever Hellenes and Barbarians reside – a metropolis which draws and binds together the ends of the West and the East'.[31]

The triumphant rhetoric of rebuilding was, however, quite different from the reality.[32] The shape and the scale of the city had changed, with an accompanying shift in focus. During the Palaiologan period, for example,

[26] Jolivet-Lévy, 'La peinture', pp. 23–28. [27] Boeck, *The Bronze*, p. 202.

[28] Gregoras, *Historia Byzantina*, IV.2, p. 88. [29] Boeck, *The Bronze*, p. 203.

[30] Swift, 'The Latins', pp. 458–474; Jacoby, 'The Urban', pp. 285–286.

[31] Gregoras, *Historia Byzantina*, VII.12, p. 276, II. 11–15 as translated and quoted in Angelov, 'Asia and Europe', p. 56.

[32] Boeck, *The Bronze*, p. 203.

the emperors and the elite preferred the north-western part of Constantinople, visiting the historical core of the city infrequently.[33] The Blachernai palace in the north-west became the principal imperial residence. The emperors were expected to visit Hagia Sophia once a year on the Feast of the Dormition of the Virgin, and for the royal coronations, but the imperial religious ceremonies in the Palaiologan era were instead celebrated mostly in the Blachernai basilica.[34]

The fortunes of artistic production, however, were not so bleak. Despite the fact that the empire, like the city, was greatly reduced in size from its earlier heights under Justinian (r. 527–565) and Basil II (r. 976–1018), the Palaiologan emperors proved to be prodigious patrons of culture. They were emulated in this by many other wealthy families of the time – in the Peloponnese, for example, and by other dynasties with imperial pretentions in Trebizond and Epirus.

With regard to wider artistic production, although there were regions such as Attica and Boetia that did not blossom and seem to have produced low-skilled and presumably poorly paid artists, painting of a high aesthetic value also appeared beyond the borders of the Byzantine Empire itself. In Bulgaria and Serbia, for example, considerable effort and expense went into building, endowing, and decorating churches – with craftsmen and artists from Constantinople and Thessaloniki being hired to create high-quality religious art. Mural ensembles in Kurbinovo, Studenica, Ivanovo, Sopočani, Ohrid and elsewhere that date from the late twelfth century onwards point to common Orthodox religious and cultural heritage being shared across territories that were politically distinct and sometimes competitive.[35]

The involvement and independence of aristocratic patrons also becomes pronounced. In Metochites'[36] time, the more renowned and wealthy aristocrats also became donors, who began to rival the scale and quality of imperial patronage. Some of them endeavoured to build churches or monasteries in order to be immortalised, sometimes failing to visually acknowledge the reigning emperor. At the Chora, for example, there is no representation of the emperor.[37] This phenomenon was a result of the weakened central power in Constantinople and the fragmentation of the countryside.

The renovation of the Chora by Metochites was one of a number of contemporary building initiatives aimed at reversing the damage that had been done to Constantinople by the Crusader attack of 1203–1204 and during the subsequent Latin occupation. This rebuilding programme was started by Michael VIII Palaiologos (1258–1282)[38] and continued by his son

[33] Boeck, *The Bronze*, p. 207. [34] Berger, 'Imperial', p. 84; Boeck, *The Bronze*, p. 207.
[35] Grabar, 'The Artistic', p. 4. [36] *PLP*, no. 17982.
[37] Magdalino, 'Theodore Metochites', p. 174. [38] *PLP*, no. 21528.

Andronikos II (1282–1328).[39] These public works of repair were funded by the emperors themselves and included projects repairing Hagia Sophia, the church of St Paul at the Orphanage, the church of the Holy Apostles, and the statue of Justinian at the Augousteion, according to Nikephoros Gregoras,[40] who called the Constantinople of his day 'the Queen of Cities'.[41] As Nelson has noted, however, Gregoras does not mention any renovation of the Chora in this period;[42] perhaps because of its remote location or because it was not an imperial project.

However, although Gregoras does not mention Metochites' work at the Chora, it is clear from Metochites' own words that he was inspired by a similar attitude to Constantinople and its rebuilding. For Metochites, Constantinople was a perfect ideal – still the world capital in his time, despite disaster and decline.[43] He describes the city as 'doubtlessly the most central and most beautiful (place) of the whole oikumene'.[44] And with regard to its churches, Metochites describes the city as full of churches dedicated to the Theotokos, which she presents as guards under her command throughout the divine *polis* (city) of Constantine.[45] It is in this context that Metochites' endowment of the Chora belongs.

Understanding the Chora

As has been said, the Chora is one of the most-published Byzantine churches, which is particularly fortunate given the current lack of access to its treasures. For a reader who wishes to appreciate its images more fully, some of the best illustrated volumes are those of Underwood,[46] Mango and Ertug,[47] Klein, Ousterhout, and Pitterakis,[48] and Studer-Karlen.[49] There are many others. Some of the Chora's images, particularly the most famous ones, can also be found online.

However, there are still many aspects of the Chora yet to be fully explored and appreciated, and this present Element seeks, along with presenting more familiar material, to highlight some areas previously little-studied or

[39] *PLP*, no. 21436; Talbot, 'The Restoration', pp. 243–261; Talbot, 'Building Activity'.
[40] Gregoras, *Historia Byzantina*, I, pp. 273–277. [41] Ibidem, IV.2, pp. 87–88, ll. 23–23.
[42] Nelson, 'The Chora', p. 68. [43] Magdalino, 'Theodore Metochites', p. 184.
[44] Cod. Vind. phil. gr. 95, f. 239v: . . . ὅτι τῆς μὲν ὅλης οἰκουμένης τὸ μεσαίτατον ἀναμφηρίστως καὶ κάλλιστον. See Rhoby, 'Theodoros', p. 81.
[45] Magdalino, 'Theodore Metochites', p. 181.
[46] Underwood, *The Kariye Djami*; Underwood, P. A. (ed.), *The Kariye Djami: Studies in the Art of Kariye Djami and Its Intellectual Background* (Princeton: Princeton University, 1975).
[47] Mango C. and A. Ertug, Chora: Scroll of Heaven (Istanbul: Ertug & Kocabiyik, 2000).
[48] Klein, H., R. Ousterhout, and B. Pittarakis (eds.), *The Kariye Camii Reconsidered* (Istanbul: İstanbul Araştırmaları Enstitüsü, 2011); Ousterhout, *Finding a Place*.
[49] Studer-Karlen, M. (ed.), *Biography of a Landmark: The Chora Monastery/ Kariye Camii in Constantinople/ Istanbul from Late Antiquity to the 21st Century* (Leiden: Brill, 2023).

under-emphasised. Some of these will be introduced in this section, which aims to offer the reader useful interpretative tools to help them understand the Chora and its context.

The Dedication of the Chora

One important question in understanding the Chora and its artwork is very simple, but not as straightforward as it might seem at first glance. To whom was the church dedicated? It is usually referred to, as has been said, as 'Saint Saviour in the Chora', that is, dedicated to Christ. However, many scholars also acknowledge a dual dedication.[50] In the twelfth century, an Athonite manuscript containing the *Vita* of the founder of the original monastery, the monk Theodoros (b. 477), talks about a small 'cell' or hermitage with a church (κελλίον μικρὸν σὺν βραχυτάτη ἐκκλησία), which it connects with the 'illustrious Charisius' after whom the Charisius Gate of Constantinople was named.[51] It is even possible that 'Chora', rather than simply meaning 'in the countryside', as generally assumed, may be a corruption of 'Charisius'. The fifth-century *Vita* says, moreover, that Theodoros dedicated the monastery to the Theotokos, the Mother of God. This dual dedication would certainly fit with the decoration of the Chora as we know it, particularly the repeated idea of Christ as 'Land of the Living' and Mary as 'Container of the Uncontainable'. It is my contention that the primary dedication of the Chora was in fact to the Theotokos; while that is contentious, the aspects of the Church that suggest at the very least a parallel dedication to the Theotokos will be explored throughout this Element.

Benefactors and Connections: Beyond Metochites

The Chora has always been, understandably, particularly strongly associated with Theodore Metochites, because of his extensive endowment of the Church and its decoration in the early fourteenth century (see Figure 1). However, I would argue that this has led to a neglect of many other aspects of the Church and its history; too much has been interpreted simply in connection with Metochites. Underwood, for example, assumed that all the tombs in the *parekklesion* (south chapel) were connected with Metochites, but without explaining who the people buried there were – except for Michael Tornikes and his wife, buried under the arcosolium that contained Tomb D – or their connection with Metochites.

As has already been seen, even before Metochites' time, the figures associated with the Chora were not insignificant, including as they did Maria Doukaina

[50] Ousterhout, 'Introduction', p. 9 with previous bibliography.

[51] Cod. 13, f. 175v-189v in the Library of Pantokrator monastery. Gedeon, 'Θεόδωρος', pp. 19–23.

Figure 1 *Donor Portrait*, Metochites donates a model of the Chora church to Christ, fourteenth-century mosaic in the inner narthex of the Chora. Photo: Author

and the *sebastokrator* Isaak – respectively mother-in-law and brother of Alexios I. However, the full extent of the connections between the Chora and the world around, whether through people or places, has yet to be fully explored.

In terms of the human element, clearly the tombs to be found in the Church, primarily in the *parekklesion* but also elsewhere, are of major importance. The precise dating of the tombs and the identification, as far as possible, of their owners are crucial to understanding Constantinopolitan aristocratic and spiritual life. Various suggestions regarding identification have been made over the years. I made my own contribution to this in 2020 with a discussion of funerals in the *parekklesion* and the presence there of Asan family tombs.[52] A year later, Nicholas Melvani, independent of my research, also suggested that the erection of the funeral structures (arcosolia) was more gradual than previously thought and reflected shifting patronal rights among different aristocratic families, particularly tombs of a branch of the Raoul-Asan clan, connected with the Palaiologoi and Dermokaites families, in the outer narthex.[53]

[52] Moutafov, *Богородица*, pp. 90–140.

[53] Melvani, 'The Last Century', p. 1235; Bacci, 'Tomb G', p. 114 refers to both studies in chronological order.

My contention is that the key to understanding many of the Chora funerary monuments can be found in an epitaph written by the fourteenth-century poet Manuel Philes, commissioned by the Grand Primikarios[54] Isaak Asan for his mother, Eirene Asanina Komnene Palaiologina (1260–1306), daughter of Michael VIII Palaiologos and wife of Ivan Asan III. When clues from this epitaph are combined with other clues from the Church itself and from what is known of the aristocratic dynasties of the time, it is possible to build up a picture of a set of aristocratic connections revolving around the Chora, stemming from the Asan dynasty but linked with the Palaiologoi, Raoul, and Dermokaites families. Figure 2 gives my identification of the individuals associated with the tombs in the *parekklesion*, and my discussion of the Tombs themselves will focus on explaining my interpretation, although mention will also be made of alternative theories.

This is not, however, to downplay completely the role of Metochites himself, whose role and connection with the Chora will always remain of great significance. Given the importance of the funerary aspect of the *parekklesion* he built, researchers have long asked: where did Theodore Metochites, the prime mover in the renovation of the Chora, himself plan to wait to be raised from the dead? There has long been strong speculation about Tomb A in this regard, but in my discussion of the *parekklesion*, I will present an alternative theory: that he in fact intended the *diakonikon*, which he also remoulded, to be his resting place.

The Chora's connections to the world around, however, are not purely through people; they also include physical and cultic elements that connect the foundation with important aspects of the life and culture of the city. Iconographically, as will be seen, there appear to be connections with various monuments and cults in Constantinople. For example, the *Deesis* in the inner narthex shows Christ as Christ *Chalkites*, connected with the image of Christ on the Chalke Gate of the imperial palace. A Virgin of the Blachernitissa type is represented on the inner wall of the arch of the main entrance, connecting the Chora to the Palace of Blachernai and the cult of the Theotokos Blachernitissa. The tomb of the Despotes Demetrios, with its image of the Virgin as *Zoodochos Pege* (Life-giving Fountain), connects with the monastery of Zoodochos Pege and its cult. Connections with Hagia Sophia itself, the Pammakaristos church, the cult of Sts Sergius and Bacchus associated with the church known as Little Hagia Sophia, and the cult of Sts Floros and Lauros can also be detected.[55] All this makes me regard the Chora as a significant cultic centre, a religious and cultural nexus, and think that it probably housed miraculous icons and relics, which raises exciting possibilities about the role of the monastery in the religious and cultural life of the city.

[54] Title of a high Byzantine official, clerk, also used in the West for Papal representatives.

[55] Ousterhout, 'The Virgin', pp. 91–109; Ousterhout, 'Contextualizing', p. 244, fig. 7; Ousterhout, 'Reading', p. 100; Studer-Karlen, 'Walking', p. 51.

Figure 2

Genealogical relation of the Palaiologoi's and Asan's images and burials in the annexes of the Chora

Deesis: Maria Palaiologina, illegitimate daughter of Michael VIII Palaiologos

Tomb A: Eirene Asanina Komnene Palaiologina (1260–1306), half sister of Maria Palaiologina and wife of Ivan Asan III

Tomb B: Constantine Palaiologos Asan, son of Eirene Asanina Palaiologina and Ivan Asan III

Tomb C: Isaak Palaiologos Asan, son of Eirene Asanina Palaiologina and Ivan Asan III

Tomb D: Michael Asan Komnenos Tornikes Palaiologos, son of Constantine Asan and grandson of Ivan Asan III

Tomb E: Eirene Asanina Raoulina Palaiologina, wife of Andronikos Asan, son of Isaak Asan, great granddaughter of Ivan Asan III

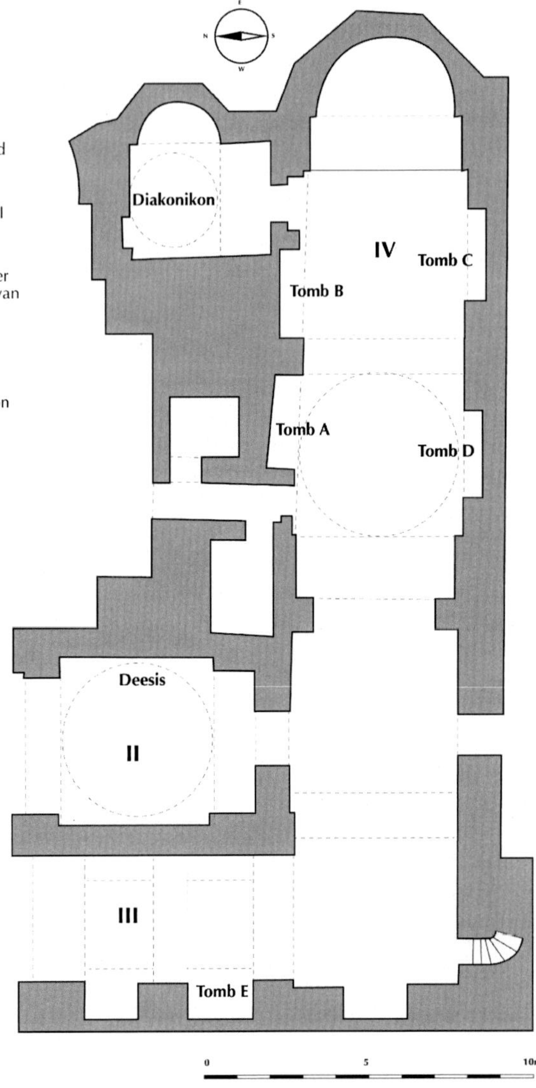

Figure 2 Genealogical positioning of the tombs in the annexes of the Chora, designed by Maya Lacheva

An Elusive Connection: Maria Palaiologina, ms. Dujčev Gr 177, and the Chora

The donor of one of the Chora's most well-known images, the imposing *Deesis* in the inner narthex, was a certain Maria Palaiologina, otherwise known as the nun Melania. She herself is depicted in the mosaic she commissioned. Not only is she a significant figure in her own right, but she is also connected with a manuscript that has great significance for our understanding of the Chora. Since this manuscript will frequently be referred to in describing the decorative scheme of the church, the manuscript, Maria herself, and Maria's connection with the Chora deserve introduction.

Maria/Melania was an illegitimate daughter of Michael VIII Palaiologos (r. 1258/1261–1282), and half-sister to Andronikos II.[56] She was married to the Mongolian khan of Bagdad, Abax; in the *Deesis* inscription, she is described as 'lady of the Mongols, nun Melane' ([. . . Ἀ]νδ(ρον)ίκου τοῦ Πα|λαιολόγου ἡ κυρὰ τῶν| Μουγουλίων Μελάνη| ἡ μοναχή)[57] – . . . *of Andronikos Palaiologos, Lady of the Mongols(?), the nun Melania* (see Figure 3). She was a distant relative of Isaak Komnenos, and through a series of marriages also distantly related to Metochites. In 1282, she returned to Constantinople and became a nun, re-founding the monastery of the Theotokos Panagiotissa c. 1285, known as the Mouchliotissa ('Our Lady of Mongols'?).[58]

Maria's connection with the Chora is unclear. It has been suggested that 'she may have also sponsored some repairs', but there is no evidence of this.[59]

Figure 3 Maria Palaiologina as the nun Melania from the *Deesis*, detail, fourteenth-century mosaic in the inner narthex of the Chora monastery. Photo: Author

[56] *PLP*, no. 21395. [57] Underwood, 'Some problems', p. 251.
[58] Ryder, 'The Despoina', pp. 71–102. [59] Ousterhout, *Finding a Place*, p. 29.

It is believed that she may have transformed the south bay of the Chora inner narthex into her own private chapel because of her imperial lineage and family ties with Metochites, since his daughter married John Palaiologos, the emperor's nephew.[60] However, for Maria's relationship to the Chora, there are only two definite pieces of evidence: one is the mosaic of her in the *Deesis*; the other is a manuscript.

This manuscript, Cod. Dujčev Gr 177, dates to the eleventh century. It is a luxuriously bound volume, including the Gospels and a number of further texts.[61] Fragments of the purple robe, or *peplum*, used for the binding of the codex can still be found on the wooden inside front and inside back covers.[62] Later in its history, the manuscript appeared in the library of the Monastery of St John the Forerunner, Serres, to reappear in the twentieth century in the collection of manuscripts kept at the Prof. Ivan Dujčev Centre for Slavo-Byzantine Studies, University of Sofia.[63]

One of the texts contained in the manuscript is a dedicatory poem referring to Maria Palaiologina and her relationship with the Chora. This poem, in Greek edition and English translation, can be found in Appendix 1 of this Element. It is included in full because of its importance in reconstructing the Chora's wider context, providing information about a local cult of the early fourteenth century.[64] The introductory lines to the poem are of particular significance: Mary is referred to as Δέσποιναν καὶ Παρθένον καὶ Θεομήτορα τὴν Χωρινὴν: 'Lady and Virgin and Mother of God *of the Chora*', indicating a local cult associated with the monastery. According to the poem, which is expressed in the first person, the manuscript in question, suitably adorned, was donated to the Chora by Maria – here described as 'Empress of the whole Orient' – in gratitude for the intervention of the Theotokos, again supporting the idea of a local cult.

That there is a connection between Cod. Dujčev Gr 177, Maria, and the Chora is therefore clear. What is less well known is how much the connection contributes to our understanding of the artwork, hagiography, and epigraphy of the Chora, through the poem itself but also through another text the manuscript includes, a *menologion* (see Figure 4).

With regard to the poem, there may well be connections between it and the decoration of the Chora and another key figure, Manuel Philes. I believe that

[60] Talbot, 'Building Activity', p. 336.

[61] It is usually described as a Greek *Tetraevangelium cum catenis* of 246 fol. from the thirteenth century; see Džurova, 'La décoration', pp. 45–59.

[62] Given that Maria's *peplum* would have been large enough to bind more than one manuscript, there may exist other manuscripts where it was also used in the binding.

[63] For the manuscript, see Teteriatnikov, 'The Place', pp. 165–180.

[64] Teteriatnikov, 'The Dedication of the Chora', pp. 194–196.

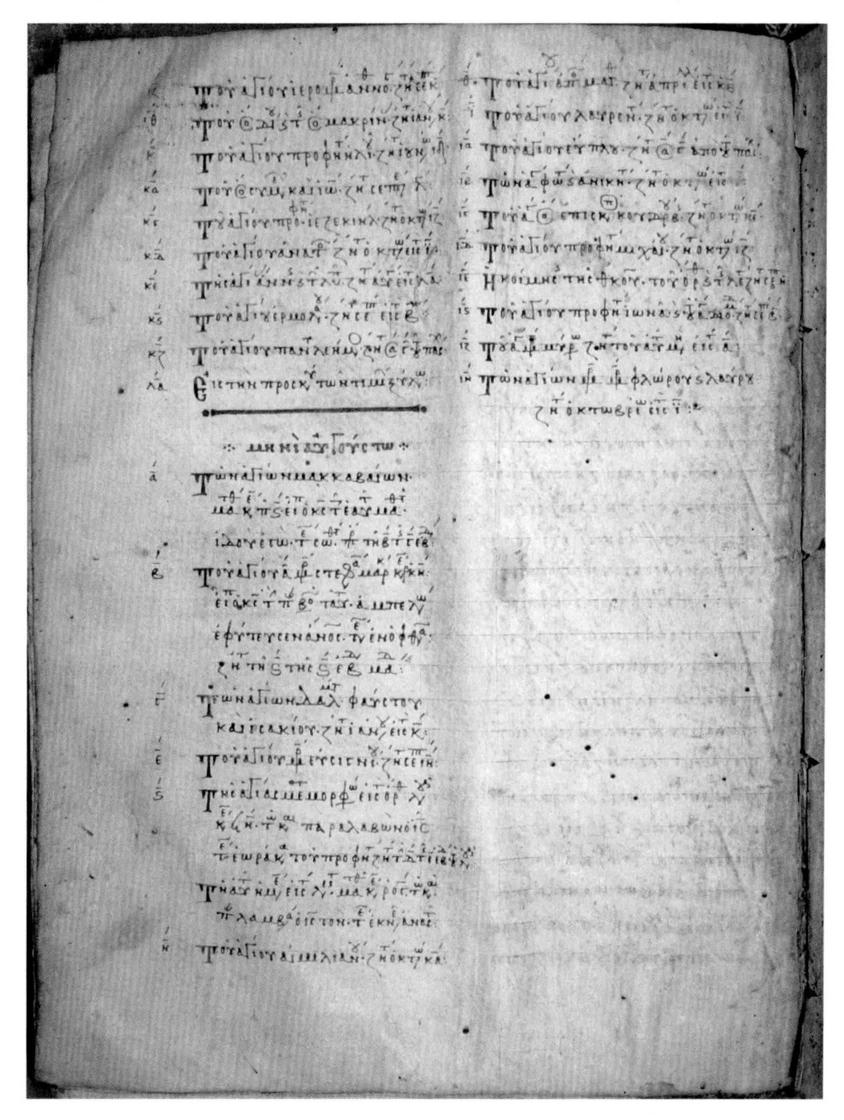

Figure 4 Feasts of July and August from the Menologion in Cod. Dujčev Gr 177, f. 13 v. Photo credit: Centre Ivan Dujčev

most contemporary commentators have never seen the manuscript itself, using instead the text published in 1894, rather than working with the original.[65] Working on the manuscript *de viso* shows that the poem is laid out in a similar manner to the layout of the epitaph for Tornikes which appears in the *parekklesion* of the Chora (Tomb D), which will be

[65] Papageorgiou, 'Αἱ Σέρραι', pp. 326–327.

commented on in what follows; that is, the verses are written from left to right, two in the same line, although they are not separated by three vertical dots as in the lunette of Tomb D. Yet another specificity of the text in Cod. Dujčev Gr 177 is that the entire poem is written in a red pigment, but in the place of verse 27, there is a mark in black pointing to the verso of the folio of the manuscript, 245 v, where in another hand and black ink is written: Χώραν καλεῖν εἴωθεν ἅπας τὸν δόμον – (*Everyone is accustomed to call the house Chora*); this indicates that the line was included later, when the manuscript was no longer kept at the Chora, and therefore the connection was no longer self-evident (see Figures 5 and 6). This is why the sentence is in brackets in the edition.

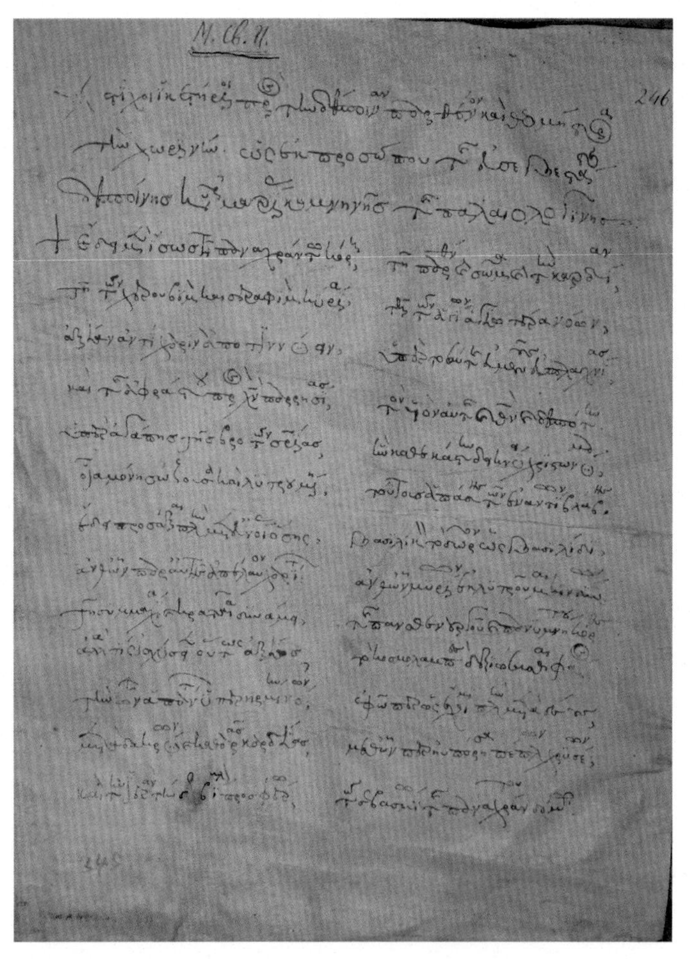

Figure 5 Poem of Maria Palaiologina for the Virgin of the Chora, Cod. Dujčev Gr 177, f. 246 r. Photo credit: Centre Ivan Dujčev

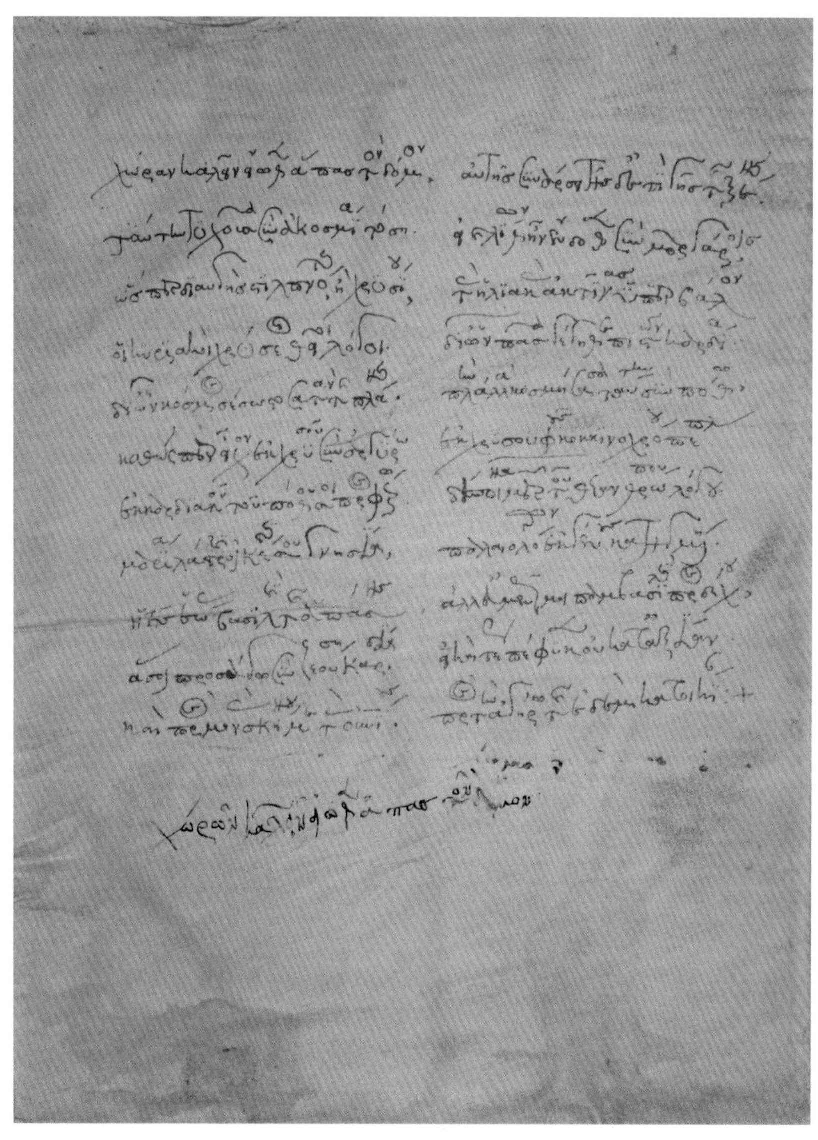

Figure 6 Poem of Maria Palaiologina for the Virgin of the Chora (continuation of the previous), Cod. Dujčev Gr 177, f. 246 v. Photo credit: Centre Ivan Dujčev

It has already been noticed that the poem relating to Maria Palaiologina bears obvious similarities to the works of Manuel Philes:[66] for example, the image of Heaven, the Sun, Earth, the idea of the royal lineage, the usage of

[66] Talbot, 'The Female', p. 272.

God Word (*Logos*) from the epitaph for the Despotes Demetrios, etc. The main character of this dodecasyllabic poem is Maria, but it would seem that the author is likely to have been Philes, which would make sense given that, as will be seen, there is undoubtedly a strong connection between Philes and the donors of the Chora. If this is the case, here we probably have Philes' autograph. On the other hand, a missing line added by someone else's hand suggests the existence of at least one more manuscript containing the full version of the poem.

Another key feature of Cod. Dujčev Gr 177 manuscript Gr 177 is that its opening contains a short *menologion*.[67] This *menologion* provides the feast days of the saints, which, in my opinion, have been used in shaping the hagiological component of the iconographic programme of the Chora. The evidence from the *menologion* is mentioned where relevant later in the descriptions of the iconography. A number of illustrations are also given.

Presentation of the Monument

The Architectural Type of the Church

The architectural structure of the Church of the Chora during the time of Maria Doukaina (c. 1077–1081) must have been a cross-in-square with four columns, covered by a large central dome on a high drum, belonging to the most common and popular architectural type at the time. Other examples of this type in Constantinople include the Pammakaristos (Church of the Theotokos Pammakaristos, the All-blessed Mother of God), now the Fethiye Camii; the church of St Theodosia or Christ Euergetes (Christ Benefactor), now the Gül Camii; and the Kyriotissa (Church of the Theotokos Kyriotissa), now the Kalenderhane Camii. This design is sometimes called the 'atrophied Greek-cross plan'.[68] It forms a cross with equal and relatively short arms, and was deemed more stable, creating a more spacious interior.

However, the development of the *naos* (nave) also owes much to the repairs of the *sebastokrator* Isaak Komnenos (c. 1120). The damage the church suffered (collapse of the apses), probably due to an earthquake or a crack in the foundations, called for significant repairs, during which a remodelling was carried out. The wide, central apse, semicircular on the inside and five-sided externally, was built at this time. The columns were replaced by the massive piers, which gives the main body of the fragmented interior space a bulky appearance but serves to support the large dome. The visual effect is, moreover, alleviated by the rich decoration of the coloured marbles and mosaics.

---

[67] A *menologion* is a calendrical liturgical book containing short *Lives* of saints.

[68] Ousterhout, *Finding a Place*, p. 23.

The appearance of the main church as seen nowadays is the result of the further repairs carried out by Theodore Metochites in the early fourteenth century, most probably again necessitated by the unstable foundations. During Metochites' renovation, the middle-Byzantine core of the structure remained essentially unaltered. The inner narthex with its dome was built, an outer narthex and the *parekklesion* (south chapel) – also domed – were added, and the north passage took its final form, with a gallery. On the eastern side, the two small side apses of the *pastophoria*,[69] and possibly a belfry, were added.[70]

The Chora church, covering as it does only 742.5 m², is not as large as other Byzantine churches in Constantinople, such as Hagia Sophia, the Pantokrator, and the Pammakaristos. This is most probably because it was originally built outside the city walls. However, the lack of monumental size is outweighed by the beauty of its interior.

The building is divided into three main areas: double narthex (outer 4 m × 23.30 m, inner 4 m × 18 m); *naos* (nave: 10.5 m × 15 m); and *parekklesion* (south chapel: 29 m long). The edifice is covered by six domes: two cover the corners of the inner narthex, another one crowns the *parekklesion*, while the central one covers the *naos* and two further domes cover the east corner bays.

The Decoration of the Chora

After 1300, the second Palaiologan artistic period (c. 1300–1330) dominates Byzantine art. The main characteristics of this artistic period are the harmonic dimensions and classical plasticity, combined with elegance, free of the stress on size and bulk that were characteristic of the heavy style of the end of the thirteenth century. Architectural depth helps to create a special effect in spatial expression, while the wider use of still life in background and graphic details creates a sense of familiarity. Against a backdrop of the dramatically shrinking borders of the imperial state, notwithstanding the loss of almost the entirety of Asia Minor, the Byzantine intelligentsia sought an outlet for expression in sophisticated art.

Metochites' structural additions to the Chora church – the *pastophoria*, north annexe, narthexes, and *parekklesion* – were all decorated with richly veined and multi-coloured marble according to the Constantinopolitan tradition. It is, however, the mosaics in the main church and the frescoes in the side chapel that make the Chora such a significant monument of the Palaiologan period, due to their unique iconography, one of the best examples of Constantinopolitan art

[69] The two chambers of the church building used as sacristies: *diakonikon* (south) and *prothesis* (north).

[70] Ousterhout, *The Architecture*; Mango, *Byzantinische*, figs. 263–265; Krautheimer, *Early Christian*, table 187; Müller-Wiener, '*Bildlexikon*', figs. 156–162; Gioles, *Βυζαντινή*, pp. 94–95.

of the period. They testify to the high quality of artistic production, as well as providing insight into the ideology of the period and the rebirth of classical studies, all characteristic of the so-called Palaiologan Renaissance.[71]

The extant decorations of the Church include the mosaics in the *naos*, inner narthex, and outer narthex, and the memorial mosaics and mural decoration in the *parekklesion*. In what follows, I will give an account of the decoration in each of these sections of the church. For the two narthexes and the *parekklesion*, I will begin with the decoration of the ceiling, moving down to the lower registers, following accepted hierarchal arrangements.

As explained earlier, the *menologion* in Cod. Dujčev Gr 177 offers insights into the iconographic programme followed in the decoration of the Chora. In my descriptions of the images, I provide the dates of the feast days of some of the saints as well as indicating how they appear in the *menologion*, as some relationships between the choices and their positioning in the church and the liturgy of the months have come to my notice.

A further point to mention is the importance of Dionysius of Phourna and the tradition of *Hermeneiai*. In attempting to reconstruct the iconographical programme of the Chora – for instance, the groupings of Byzantine saints – many eminent scholars, including Ousterhout, have recourse to Dionysius' *Hermeneia*, which is a pre-modern artists' manual written in Greek;[72] a humble eastern equivalent of Cennino Cennini's 'libro dell'arte', for Orthodox iconography. Dionysius drew principally on Palaiologan models and the artwork of Mount Athos, mentioning particularly the churches decorated by the legendary Manuel Panselinos.[73] Later *Hermeneiai* from the Balkans are heavily indebted to Dionysius, but although they post-date Palaiologan models (many manuscripts date from the eighteenth and nineteenth centuries), they too can and should be used to help reconstruct earlier iconographic programmes of mural painting, decipher inscriptions, and to understand the meaning of the medieval titles given to the Theotokos, to Christ, and to the saints and martyrs.

Finally, the Greek inscriptions in the following pages are offered with my reading of their epigraphic edited text in Greek and additional translation into English in italics when the Greek differs from the generally accepted title of the scene. Biblical quotations are from the King James Version. Most impressively, the inscriptions are very correctly rendered, which suggests that they were copied on site from a manuscript. The few mistakes are highlighted with '*sic!*'.

For the sake of brevity, comments on the iconographic specifics, parallels, and theological connections are kept to a minimum.

[71] Richter, 'Abendländische Malerei', pp. 205–206; Kondakov, *Мозаики*, pp. 21–23; Boeck, *The Bronze*, p. 205.

[72] Ousterhout, 'The Art', p. 30. [73] Dionysius of Phourna, *Έρμηνεία*, p. 3.

I. *Naos* (nave)

Three mosaics survive in the *naos*. They frame the chancel in the following order: (1) Christ (Pantokrator); (2) Theotokos and Child; and, above the entrance to the *naos*, or rather on its west wall, (3) the Dormition (see Figure 7).

1. Christ (Pantokrator) – no extant inscriptions around the nimbus, and the open book in his right hand is inscribed: Δεῦτε| πρός με| πάντες οἱ κοπι|ῶντες κ(αὶ) πεφορ|τισμένοι,| κἀγὼ ἀ(ναπαύσω ὑμᾶς) – *Come unto me, all ye that labour and are heavy laden, and I will give you rest* (Matt. 11:28). This quote identifies Christ as Pantokrator, even though he is not depicted in the dome.
2. Theotokos and Child – Μή(τη)ρ Θ(εο)ῦ| ἡ Χώρα τοῦ Ἀχωρήτου| Ἰ(ησοῦ)ς Χ(ριστὸ)ς – *Mother of God the Container (Chora) of the Uncontainable| Jesus Christ.* Although inscribed as 'Container of the Uncontainable', this *naos* image of Mary is a common type known as the Hodegetria (see Figure 8). This pattern is probably also true of the Christ image, which iconographically is of the Pantokrator type, but standing full length and was

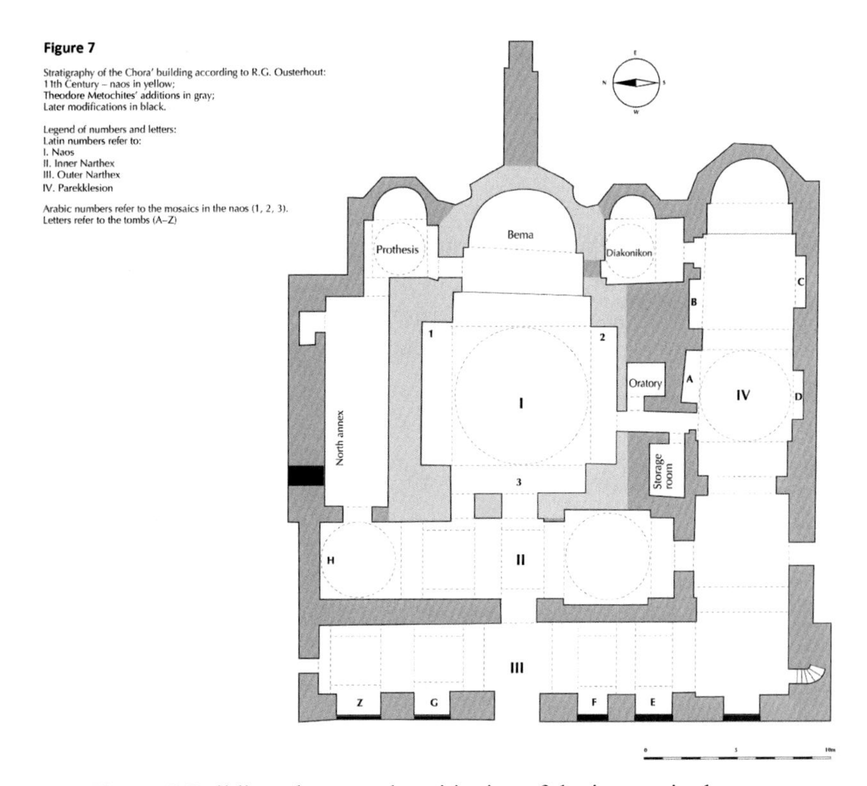

Figure 7 Building phases and positioning of the images in the *naos*, designed by Maya Lacheva

Figure 8 Virgin Mary with Child as the Container of the Uncontainable, fourteenth-century mosaic in the *naos* of the Chora. Photo: Author

probably inscribed 'Land of the Living' like the image above the entrance to the inner narthex.

3. Dormition of the Theotokos – Ἡ κ[οίμ]ησης τῆς Θ(εοτό)κου, Ἰ(ησοῦ)ς Χ(ριστὸ)ς. This is exactly how the Dormition is presented in Cod. Dujčev Gr 177, f. 13 v: ιε΄ (μηνὶ αὐγοῦστου) ἡ κοίμησις τῆς Θ(εοτό)κου – *15 August, Dormition of the Theotokos.*

Other than these three surviving mosaics, it is not known what further scenes and individuals were depicted in the *naos*. A strong possibility is that it was decorated with a cycle of the Passion of Christ, along with the evangelists and some of the monastic saints, possibly the patrons of local monasteries.

The pairs of monumental marble doors between the inner narthex and *naos* are also worth mentioning. These are spolia.[74] Unfortunately, their provenance is unknown, although it has been suggested they came from Hagia Sophia.

II. Inner narthex (see Figure 9)

The inner narthex contains the famous *Donor Portrait* of Theodore Metochites and the *Deesis*, as well as genealogies of Christ and the Virgin and extended sets of scenes from the *Lives* of both. Many of these scenes and figures would have been familiar to a contemporary audience, being taken either from the Bible or from well-known sources; in the case of the *Life of the Virgin*, the primary source of the extra-Biblical material is the apocryphal *Protoevangelium of James*.

[74] Spolia: repurposed stones, architectural elements, or decorative sculptures reused in new monuments.

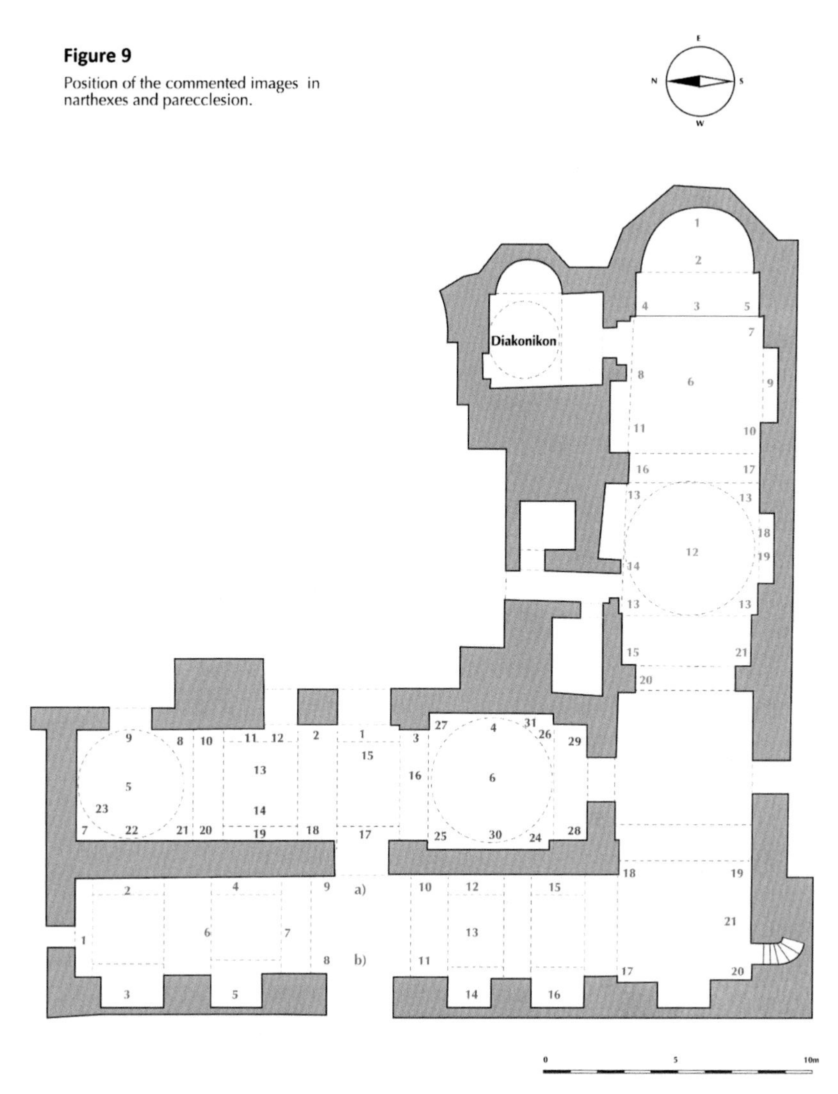

Figure 9 Positioning of the images in the narthexes and the *parekklesion*, designed by Maya Lacheva

1. *Metochites' Donor Portrait*. This mosaic, in the inner narthex, above the door to the *naos*, shows Metochites presenting a small model of the Chora church to an enthroned Christ. Metochites is shown wearing a tall hat in a style fashionable in the early fourteenth century.

The inscription on donor's left says: + Ὁ κτή|τωρ λο|γοθέ|της τοῦ γε|νικοῦ Θεό|δωρος| ὁ Μετο|χίτης (*The Benefactor and Minister of the Treasury Theodore Metochites*).

As discussed earlier, there is some debate as to whether the Chora was dedicated to Christ or to the Theotokos, or perhaps both. This mosaic panel showing Metochites giving a model of the church to Christ does not automatically mean that the church was dedicated to the latter. In the third quarter of the fourteenth century, for example, the founder of the Church of the Panagia Phorbiotissa Asinou (Cyprus) is represented offering a model of a building to Christ, but the church was in fact dedicated to the Theotokos.[75] This is a particularly interesting parallel, given that an early source suggests the Chora was dedicated to the Theotokos. The image of Theodore in proskynesis before Christ is in any case striking: a unique depiction of the donor in two roles, as both kneeling supplicant and benefactor.[76]

The image of the church being offered is, however, also commendable. All similar models of buildings are highly conventional in Byzantine art and this particular one is also symbolic. The edifice has three entrances and three domes, which does not correspond with the six domes of Metochites' church. The model is also quite symmetrical, unlike the actual church. One could perhaps assume that this is usual for the arbitrary nature of vision in Orthodoxy. However, it has been shown that the pitchers depicted in the mosaic of the *Marriage at Cana* in the Chora are accurate representations of contemporary Byzantine vessels;[77] and Metochites' hat and clothes also follow real models of that period.

Is such apparent artistic clumsiness possible in the case of the donor's portrait, when this building was 'an extension of the founder's self, and founder's palace and private estate – his *oikos*'?[78] Leading scholars have argued that the image above the entrance to the *naos* shows Metochites presenting the church – that is, the *naos*, but not the *parekklesion* and the narthexes.[79] This I find hard to accept, because the main church was not built by Metochites and has two entrances, not three; and it is well known that Metochites was personally invested, emotionally and reputationally, as well as financially, in the church, so it is unlikely he would have downplayed his achievement.

I would like to offer an alternative explanation for the appearance of the church in the *Donor Portrait*. As has been seen, the name 'Chora', while on one level meaning simply 'in the country', also connects with the Christ and Mary. Before one approaches the *Donor Portrait* in the inner narthex, one has already stepped past the outer narthex mosaics of Christ as the 'Land (Chora) of the Living' and Mary as 'Container (Chora) of the Uncontainable', expressing the double dedication already mentioned. On the other hand, the iconographical programme of the *parekklesion* burial chapel, as will be seen, symbolises the 'Land of the Dead',

[75] Teteriatikov, 'The Dedication of the Chora', p. 205. [76] Studer-Karlen, 'Walking', p. 50.
[77] Bakirtzis, *Βυζαντινά*, p. 93, pls. 24, 40b. [78] Magdalino, 'Theodore Metochites', p. 170.
[79] Underwood, *The Kariye*, I, pp. 27–28, 42–43.

who await the absolution of their sins and the Second Coming through Resurrection. That is why, I would suggest, the model of the church Theodore offers to Jesus has three domes and entrances: one for the land of the living, one for the land of the dead, and one for the land of the 'uncontainable' or of the universe.

The composition is asymmetrical, and the space opposite Metochites has been left empty; this peculiarity has not yet been satisfactorily explained.

2. *St Peter* – Ὁ Ἅγιος Πέτρος. This saint is also represented in *The Last Judgement*, *The Marriage at Cana*, and *Walking on Water.*
3. *St Paul* – Ὁ Ἅγιος Παῦλος.
4. *Deesis*. The large *Deesis* decorating the eastern wall of the inner narthex holds a significant place among the mosaics of the Chora.[80] A *Deesis* would normally contain the figures of Christ in Majesty flanked by the Theotokos and John the Baptist, but in this case, it comprises only Christ and the Theotokos.

It is a work of art executed largely in the contemporary Palaiologan style, but with archaising features, created after 1307. It has been suggested that the tomb of Maria Palaiologina, the donor of the mosaic, who became a nun with the name Melania, was underneath the *Deesis*.[81] The mosaic is, therefore, connected with funerary tradition and worship, since the Virgin Mary Μή(τη)ρ [Θεοῦ] prays for absolution of sins and the salvation of the souls of the dead. To Mary's side, there is the *sebastokrator* Isaak Komnenos (+ Ὁ υἱὸς τοῦ ὑ|ψηλοτάτου| βασιλέως| Ἀλεξίου| τοῦ Κομνηνοῦ| Ἰσαάκιος| ὁ πορ|φυρο|γέννη|τος – *son of the most exalted emperor Alexius, Isaak the porphyrogennetos*), on his knees, praying (only his head and right shoulder survive), while next to Christ, the nun Melania is also in a pose of prayer (only her face survives).

In the *Deesis* scene, the figures of Mary and Christ – Ἰ(ησοῦ)ς Χ(ριστὸ)ς| ὁ Χαλκίτη[ς] – *Jesus Christ Chalkites* – are very archaic and stylistically do not have the lightness and subtlety of most Constantinopolitan monuments of this period. It is possible that the artists were imitating an earlier model, as shown by the use of the adjective *Chalkites* ('of the Chalke Gate') in Christ's inscription; this may be a representation of the renowned icon of Christ above the Chalke Gate of the imperial palace. Christ's face shows the characteristic elements of the fourteenth-century artistic style, however the Theotokos reminds us more of the artistic tradition of the Komnenian era (1081–1184).[82] The image of Mary may also be a reference to another famous image, the imperial Hagiosoritissa, related to the relic of the *soros* (remains, but here the Holy Girdle of Mary), kept in the Chalkoprateia church in Constantinople.[83]

[80] Underwood, 'Notes', pp. 295–296 (with the earlier bibliography), and Underwood, 'The Deesis'.
[81] Schmit, *Мозаика*, pp. 39–40. [82] Lazarev, *История*, pp. 160–161.
[83] Ousterhout, *Finding a Place*, p. 45.

5. *Genealogy of Christ*. Christ Pantokrator is portrayed in a medallion in the centre of the dome in the northern bay of the inner narthex, bearing an inscription: Ἰ(ησοῦ)ς Χ(ριστὸ)ς. In the folds of the dome, the figures of the following Forefathers are represented concentrically:
   - Ἀδάμ – Adam;
   - Σὴ[θ] – Seth;
   - Μαλελὴλ – Malelel;
   - Ἰάρεδ – Jared;
   - Λάμε|χ – Lamech;
   - Σὴμ – Shem;
   - Ἰάφεθ – Jareth;
   - Ἀρφαξὰδ – Arphaxad;
   - Σάλα – Salah;
   - Ἔβερ – Eber;
   - Σεροὺχ – Seruh;
   - Ναχὼρ – Nahor;
   - Θάρ(ρ)α – Tharah;
   - Ἀβραὰμ – Abraham;
   - Ἰσαὰκ – Isaac;
   - Ἰακὼβ – Jacob;
   - Φάλεκ – Phaleg/Peleg;
   - Ραγαῦ (sic! Ῥαγὰβ) – Ragau;
   - Μαθουσά|λα(ς) – Mathousala;
   - Ἐνὼχ – Enoch;
   - Ἐνώς – Enos;
   - Ἄβελ – Abel;
   - Λευΐ – Levi;
   - Ἰούδας – Judas;
   - Ζαβουλ|ών – Zebulon;
   - Ἰσσάχαρ – Issachar;
   - Δάν – Dan;
   - Γάδ – Gad;
   - Ἀ(σ)θήρ – Asther;
   - Νεφθαλεί|μ – Nephilim;
   - Ἰωσή(φ) – Joseph;
   - Βενηαμίν (sic! Βενιαμίν) – Benjamin;
   - Φαρὲς – Pharez;
   - Ζαρᾶ – Zarah;
   - Ἐσρὼμ – Esrom.

These figures correspond to accepted hagiographical schemes as known from the *Hermeneia* of Dionysius of Phourna, but also include names that belong to the genealogy of the Virgin.

6. *The Genealogy of the Virgin*. The Virgin Mary with the Child – Μή(τη)ρ Θ (εο)ῦ – Mother of God – is portrayed in a medallion in the centre of the dome of the north bay of the inner narthex.

   In the folds of the dome kings, patriarchs and 'the righteous' are depicted as follows:
   - Δα(υὶ)δ – David;
   - Σολομὼ|ν – Solomon;
   - Ῥοβοὰμ – Roboam;
   - Ἀβιὰ – Abias;
   - Ἀσ(σ)ὰ – Asa;
   - Ἰωσαφὰτ – Josaphat;
   - Ἰωρὰμ – Joram;
   - Ὀζίας – Oziah;
   - Ἰωθὰμ – Jotham;
   - Ἄχαζ – Ahaziah;
   - Ἐζεκίας – Hezekiah;
   - Μανασσῆ|ς – Manasseh;
   - Ἀμμὼν – Ammon;
   - Ἰωσίας – Josiah;
   - Ἰεχωνίας – Jechonias;
   - Σαλαθιήλ – Salathiel;
   - Ἀνανίας – Ananiah;
   - Ἀζαρίας – Azariah;
   - Μισαὴλ – Misael;
   - Δανιὴλ – Daniel, who holds a scroll inscribed: καὶ ὁ| λίθος| ὁ πα|τάξ(ας)| τ(ὴν) εἰ|κόν(α ἐγενήθη ὄρος μέγα καὶ ἐπλήρωσε πᾶσαν τὴν γῆν) – *and the stone that smote the image became a great mountain, and filled the whole earth* (Daniel 2:35).
   - [Ἰησοῦς ὁ τοῦ] Ναυή – Joshua son of Nun;
   - Μωϋσῆς – Moses;
   - Ἀαρὼν – Aaron;
   - Ὢρ – Hur;
   - Σαμουὴλ – Samuel;
   - Ἰὼβ – Job;
   - Μελχισεδέκ – Melchizedek.

7. *The Rejection of Joachim's Offering* – Ἡ πρὸς ἐν . . . (?). Only the figure of the high priest is extant. This scene was developed as early as the eleventh

century, as is witnessed by a silver icon from Zarzma, and a century later appeared in Russian murals.[84]

8. *Joachim, Childless, Goes into the Wilderness* – Ἰωακεῖμ προσευχόμ(ενός) ἐν τῷ ὄρει μετὰ τῶν| ποιμένων – *Joachim praying with the shepherds on the mountain.* The scene is based on the Protoevangelium 1:4 and in the other monuments[85] is usually combined with the following scene, *The Annunciation to St Anne.*[86]
9. *The Annunciation to St Anne* – Ἡ Ἁ(γία) Ἄννα προσευχόμε|νη ἐν τῷ Παράδεισῳ – *St Anne Praying in Heaven.*
10. *Meeting of Joachim and Anne* – Ἡ σύλληψις τ(ῆς) Θ(εοτό)κου – *Conception of the Virgin.* Joachim and Anne are represented kissing one another, symbolising conception (ἀσπασμός). In the later tradition, this scene is simply part of the Nativity of the Most Holy Mother of God.[87] In Cod. Dujčev Gr 177, f. 11 v, this event is recorded as θ΄ (δεκεμβρίῳ) τῆς ἁγίας Ἄννης ἡ σύλληψις – *9 (December) The Conception by St Anne.* In other words, the Dujčev manuscript was not used as the source of the titles of the scenes, but only for the names of the saints and the calendar order of feasts.
11. *The Birth of the Virgin Mary* – Ἡ Γέννησις τῆς Θ(εοτό)κου. Parallels with this iconographic composition can be found in earlier and contemporary monuments in what are now Northern Macedonia and Serbia, and on Mount Athos.[88]
12. *The Virgin's First Seven Steps* – Ἡ ἑπταβηματίζουσα (Θεοτόκος) – *Heptabematizousa.* The very rare scene is based on the apocryphal Protoevangelium of James.[89] It also appears in the Church of the Virgin Peribleptos in Ohrid, and on Mt Athos in the sixteenth century.[90]
13. *The Virgin Caressed by Her Parents* – Ἡ κολακεῖα τῆς Θ(εοτό)κου – *Caresses of the Virgin.* This scene directly follows on from the *First Seven Steps of the Virgin* and is more typical of Palaiologan art in Northern Macedonia and Serbia than of the Constantinopolitan tradition.[91]
14. *The Virgin Blessed by the Priests* – Ἡ εὐλόγησις τῶν ἱερέων – *The Blessing of the Priests.*
15. *The Presentation of the Virgin in the Temple* – Τὰ Ἅγια τῶν Ἁγίων – *The Holy of the Holies.* Both the *Presentation of the Virgin in the Temple* and the *Birth of*

[84] See Lafontaine-Dosogne, 'Iconography of the Cycle', p. 167.
[85] Ohrid, Holy Apostles in Thessaloniki, Vatopedi, etc.
[86] Lafontaine-Dosogne, 'Iconography of the Cycle', p. 170. [87] Ibidem, p. 174.
[88] Ibidem, p. 175.
[89] Ibidem, p. 177. Occurrences dating earlier than the Chora have been found in San Marco, Kızıl Çukur in Cappadocia, and Ateni in Georgia.
[90] Kalokyres, *Η Θεοτόκος*, pp. 97–98.
[91] Lafontaine-Dosogne, 'Iconography of the Cycle', p. 178.

the Virgin not only illustrate essential episodes in the Infancy of the Virgin but are also important themes because they are connected with liturgical feasts that were celebrated in Byzantium with the greatest solemnity.[92]

16. *The Virgin Fed by an Angel* – Μή(τη)ρ Θ(εο)ῦ| Ἡ Θ(εοτό)κος δεχόμενη τ(ὸν) ἄρτον παρὰ τοῦ Ἀγγέλου – *Theotokos/The Most Holy Mother of God Receiving Bread from the Angel*. The motif of Mary fed by an angel is here simply a repetition of part of the scene of the *Presentation*.[93] This observation is confirmed by the presence of the feast of the Presentation of the Virgin in the Temple in Cod. Dujčev Gr 177, f. 11 v, more commonly known as κα′ (νοεμβρίῳ) τὰ εἰσόδια τῆς Π(αναγί)ας Θ(εοτό)κου, ζήτ' σεπ(τεμβρίῳ) εἰς η′ – *21 November, the Entry of the All-Holy Virgin into the Temple, see 8 September*.
17. *The Virgin's Instruction in the Temple* – Ἡ Θ(εοτό)κος διδασκόμενη ἐν τῷ ἱερῷ. The scene is almost lost but the inscription survives. Fragments of a religious building shown in the scene are believed to have been realistically represented, bearing a resemblance to an early Christian mosaic decoration.[94]
18. *The Virgin Receiving a Skein of Wool from the Temple* – ἐνέγκοντες οἱ ὑπηρέται ταῖς παρθένοις| τοῦ λαβεῖν ἔρια ἔλαχε τῃ Μα|ριάμ τῇ πορφυροῦν – *The temple assistants brought wool for the maidens to choose, and Mary took up the purple*. This rather unusual scene depicts the Protoevangelium of James, 10:1–2. The sole parallel for this in the tradition of monumental mural painting is found in the Peribleptos in Mystras.[95]
19. *Zacharias and the Twelve Rods* – Ἡ πρὸς τὰς ῥαύδους (sic! ῥάβδους) προσευχὴ – *Praying over the Rods*. This scene and the following scenes – *The Virgin Entrusted to Joseph*, *Joseph Taking the Virgin to His House* and *Joseph Taking Leave of the Virgin* – illustrate the Protoevangelium of James, 8:2–9.
20. *The Virgin Entrusted to Joseph* – Ἡ πρὸς τὸν Ἰωσὴφ παράδοσις – *Handing (the Theotokos) over to Joseph*. Most researchers believe that this scene appears due to its symbolic connection with Metochites' political career. The big age difference between Mary and Joseph is emphasised because one of Metochites' most important diplomatic missions was to arrange such a misalliance. In 1299, he was sent to negotiate the marriage of the five-year-old Simonis, daughter of Andronikos II, to the middle-aged King Stefan Uroš Milutin of Serbia (1253–1321). For this purpose, Metochites had to visit Serbia five times, and the results of his mission shocked Byzantine society and, above all, the patriarch.[96] This thesis was put

[92] Ibidem, p. 179. [93] Ibidem, p. 181. [94] Ibidem, p. 182. [95] Ibidem, p. 183.
[96] Ševčenko, 'Theodore Metochites', pp. 26–27.

forward by Ousterhout, and is widely accepted. It is significant that in the inscription, the word *παράδοσις* (handing over) is used, rather than the Greek word for entrusted.

21. *Joseph Taking Mary to His House* – Ὁ Ἰωσὴφ παραλαβῶν τὴν Θ(εοτό)κον ἀπέρ|χεται ἐν τῷ οἴκῳ αὐτοῦ – *Joseph Receiving the Theotokos and Taking Her to His House.*
22. *The Annunciation to the Virgin Mary* – Ὁ εἰς τὸ φρέαρ εὐαγγελι(σ)μός – *The Annunciation at the Well.* This scene illustrates 11:1–2 of the Protoevangelium of James. This scene is opposite the *Annunciation to St Anna.*
23. *Joseph Taking his Leave of the Virgin* – Ἰδοὺ καταλιμπάνω σε ἐν τῷ| οἴκῳ μου ἐγώ γὰρ ἀπέρχομαι οἰκοδομεῖν . . . – *see 'I am leaving you behind in my own house, for I am departing to build houses'*, a quotation from an apocryphal text of the Protoevangelium.[97] This scene closes the cycle of the Life of the Virgin, which at the Chora has a distinctive character, closer to the contemporary monuments in Northern Macedonia, in Serbia, and on Mount Athos, than to those in Mystras.[98] The only fragmentary preserved cycle of this type is in the Holy Apostles in Thessaloniki from the second quarter of the fourteenth century; the Chora's cycle stands almost alone in Byzantine art.
24. *Christ Healing a Blind and Dumb Man* – Ὁ Χ(ριστὸ)ς ἰώμεν|ος τὸν τυφλόν κ(αὶ) κωφόν (or δαιμονιζόμενον τυφλόκωφον) – *Christ Healing the (Demoniac) Blind and Dumb Man* (Matt. 12:22).[99]
25. *Christ Healing Two Blind Men* – Ὁ Χ(ριστὸ)ς ἰώμεν|ος τοὺς δύο τυφλούς (Matt. 20:30–34).
26. *Jesus Healing the Woman with the Haemorrhage* – Ὁ Χ(ριστὸ)ς ἰώμενος τὴν αἱμορροοῦσ|αν – *Christ Healing the Bleeding Woman* (Matt. 9:20–22; Mark 5:25–34; Luke 8:43–48).
27. *The Healing of Peter's Mother-in-Law* – Ὁ Χ(ριστὸ)ς ἰώμενος τὴν πενθερὰν τοῦ Πέτρου (Matt. 8:14,15; Mark 1:29–31; Luke 4:38,39).
28. *The Healing of a Young Man with Withered Hand* – Ὁ Χ(ριστὸ)ς ἰώμενος τ(ὸν) ξηρὰν ἔχοντα τὴν χειρα (Matt. 12:10–13; Mark 3: 1–5; Luke 6: 6–10).
29. *The Healing of a Leper* – Ὁ Χ(ριστὸ)ς ἰώμενος τὸν λεπρόν (Mark 1:40–42; Matt. 7:2–4; Luke 5:12–14).
30. *Christ Healing the Afflicted* – Ὁ Χ(ριστὸ)ς ἰώμενος τὰ ποικίλα πάθη τῶν νοσημάτων – *Christ Curing Every Disease and Sickness* (Luke 5:40,41; Matt. 15:30,31; Mark 1:32–34).
31. Unknown scene of healing – Ἰ(ησοῦ)ς Χ(ριστὸ)ς | Ὁ Χ(ριστὸ)ς ἰώμενος . . . – *Christ curing . . .*

[97] *Codex*, Vol. I, chapter IX, p. 210.
[98] Lafontaine-Dosogne, 'Iconography of the Cycle', p. 193.
[99] Underwood, *The Kariye*, pp. 243–302.

Burial recess H (see Figure 7)

There is one burial recess (arcosolium[100]) in the inner narthex. This is the tomb of the Despotes Demetrios Palaiologos[101] (1297–1343), son of Andronikos II and Eirene (Yolanda).

In the centre of the arcosolium are depicted: ['Ιησοῦς Χριστὸς] ἡ χώ[ρα] τῶν ζών|των – *Jesus Christ Land of Living* and Μή(τη)ρ Θ(εο)ῦ ἡ ζωο|δόχος πη|γὴ – *Mother of God Zoodochos Pege (Life-giving Fountain).*

The reference to Mary as *Zoodochos Pege* connects with another very famous Constantinopolitan cultic centre, the monastery of the Virgin Zoodochos Pege (now *Balıklı Kilisesi*). This monastery was a major site of pilgrimage, and the feast day of Zoodochos Pege was instituted on the Friday of Bright Week (the Friday following Easter). The shrine underwent a period of revival during the reign of Andronikos II Palaiologos (1282–1328),[102] whose son was then buried in the Chora, underneath an image of the Mother of God Life-giving Fountain.

Below, traces of a text in a metrical foot survive as follows:

> Ζωῆς σὺ πηγὴ ὡς [Θεο]ῦ μή(τη)ρ Λόγου·– *You are the source of life as the Mother of God, the Logos.*
>
> Δημή[τριος δ'] ἔγωγε σὸς [δοῦλος] πόθῳ – *And I am Demetrius your servant with love.*

What we have here is certainly an epitaph, invoking Mary as Zoodochos Pege. These verses were composed by Manuel Philes.[103]

Nikephoros Gregoras and John Kantakouzenos both relate that the *despotes* Demetrios, *protovestiarios* Andronikos Palaiologos, and Michael Asan, the eldest son of King Ivan Asan III of Bulgaria, were the main participants in the war waged between the Byzantines and Bulgarians during the reigns of Andronikos II and Andronikos III in 1326–1328.[104] All three of them sided, of course, with Andronikos II, and after losing the civil war, the *despotes* Demetrios returned to Constantinople and was apparently buried at the Chora, long after 1328 rather than shortly after 1320, as previously assumed.[105]

III. Outer narthex (see Figure 9)

The outer narthex includes the monumental image of Christ Pantokrator over the doorway to the inner narthex, with the image of the Virgin facing him. The rest of the decoration of the exonarthex, which includes further scenes from

[100] An arched niche containing a tomb.
[101] Underwood, *The Kariye*, I, pp. 295–299.
[102] Troupkou, 'Ο τάφος', pp. 301–317.
[103] *PLP*, no. 29817.
[104] Cantantacuzenos, *Historiarium Libri IV*, 2, 4–5; I, p. 394.
[105] Underwood, *The Kariye*, I, p. 296.

Figure 10 The Chora Church, view from the West. Photo: Dimitra Sikalidou

the life of Christ, has in many cases only partially survived, with some of the fragments bearing no inscriptions.

a) When entering the building from the west (see Figure 10), the viewer is welcomed by a monumental image of Christ Pantokrator above the door to the inner narthex. Christ is represented as a bust and holds the closed Gospel in his left hand, gesturing with the other. The inscription reads: Ἰ(ησοῦ)ς Χ(ριστό)ς| Ἡ χώρα τῶν ζώντων – *Jesus Christ, Land (Chora) of the Living*. This is one of the most frequently reproduced Byzantine mosaic images of our time, primarily because of the vivid representation of the face of Christ (see Figure 11).
b) A small pendant image of the Virgin faces Christ, on the inner wall of the outer narthex, above the main gate, and is inscribed; Μ(ήτη)ρ Θ(εο)ῦ| Ἡ χώρα τοῦ ἀχωρήτου – *Mother of God, Container (Chora) of the Uncontainable*. The Virgin here is adored by angels and represented with the Christ child (Ἰ(ησοῦ)ς Χ(ριστό)ς) in her womb. This type is commonly called Blachernitissa by art historians, because a similar icon was modelled and housed in the nearby church of Blachernai. As already described, the other image of the Virgin as 'Container of the Uncontainable', with exactly the same inscription, is in the *naos* and follows the Hodegetria type. The images of Christ and the Virgin in the outer narthex are interconnected and crucial for understanding the iconographic legacy of the Chora (see Figure 12).

Figure 11 Christ as the Land of the Living, fourteenth-century mosaic in the outer narthex of the Chora. Photo: Author

Figure 12 Virgin Mary as the Container of the Uncontainable, fourteenth-century mosaic in the outer narthex of the Chora. Photo: Author

1. *Joseph's Dream and the Journey to Bethlehem*

   (a) *Joseph's Dream* – ἰδοὺ ἄγγελος Κ(υρίο)υ κατ᾽ ὄναρ ἐφάνη αὐτῷ λέγων·| Ἰωσὴφ υἱὸς Δα(υΐ)δ, μὴ φοβηθῇς παραλαβεῖν Μαριὰμ| τὴν γυναῖκα σου· τὸ γὰρ ἐν αὐτῇ γεννηθὲν ἐκ Πν(εύματό)ς ἐστιν Ἁγίου – *behold, the angel of the Lord appeared unto him in a dream, saying, Joseph, thou son of David, fear not to take unto thee Mary thy wife: for that which is conceived in her is of the Holy Ghost* (Matt. 1:20). Μή(τη)ρ Θ(εο)ῦ is inscribed above the Theotokos. The cycle of the infancy of Christ begins with *Joseph's Dream*.[106]

(b) *Journey to Bethlehem* – Ἀνέβη δὲ καὶ Ἰωσήφ ἀπὸ τῆς Γαλιλαίας, ἐκ πόλεως| Ναζαρὲτ, εἰς τὴν Ἰουδαίαν, εἰς πόλιν Δαβὶδ, ἥτις καλεῖται| Βηθλεὲμ – *And Joseph also went up from Galilee, out of the city of Nazareth, into Judaea, unto the city of David, which is called Bethlehem* (Luke 2:4). Joseph here supports the pregnant Mary in especially realistic fashion; a rare image, a parallel for which is found on the much earlier Throne of Maximian.[107]

2. *Enrolment for Taxation* – διὰ τὸ εἶναι αὐτὸν ἐξ οἴκου καὶ πατριᾶς Δα(υΐ)δ, ἀπο| γράψασθαι σὺν Μαριὰμ τῇ μεμνηστευμένῃ| αὐτῷ γυναικί, οὔσῃ ἐγκύῳ – *Because he was of the house and the lineage of David, to be taxed with Mary his espoused wife, being great with child* (Luke 2:4–5). Here the sentence from the previous scene, the *Journey to Bethlehem*, continues, following Luke word for word. Μή(τη)ρ Θ(εο)ῦ is inscribed above the Theotokos. Especially interesting are the letters used on the scroll held by the servant of the Roman governor Quirinius: these letters are fantastical, deliberately neither Latin, Greek, nor Hebrew; apparently the painter was hesitant about the language of the census.

This scene is unique to the entire Byzantine tradition. Theodore Metochites in his capacity as the minister of the treasury is said to have made his fortune by being involved in tax collection, or therefore in corruption. This is why the tax collector in the scene is sitting on a throne wearing a tall hat like that worn by Metochites in the *Donor Portrait*. The tax collector is also said to look very much like the Metochites.[108]

In the arch, immediately above the *Enrolment for Taxation*, the following are represented:

- Ὁ Ἅγιος Μαρδάριος – St Mardarios;
- [Ὁ Ἅγιος] Αὐ[ξ]έντιος – St Auxentios;
- Ὁ Ἅγιος Εὐστράτιος – St Eustratios;
- Ὁ Ἅγιος Εὐγένιος – St Eugenios;
- Ὁ Ἅγιος Ὀρέστης – St Orestes.

These saints, in almost the same order, are recommended for representation by the Priest Daniel among the forty-two Anargyroi ('Unmercenaries', literally

[106] Lafontaine-Dosogne, 'The Cycle of the Infancy', p. 202. [107] Ibidem, p. 205.

[108] Robert Nelson referred to this scene as *Taxation with representation*: see Nelson, 'Taxation', pp. 56–82.

'without silver': saints whose good deeds were not recompensed financially).[109] Their feast day falls on 13 December. In Cod. Dujčev Gr 177, f. 11 v, this day is recorded as ιγ´ (δεκεμβρίῳ) τῶν ἁγίων μαρτύρων μαρτύρων Εὐστρατίου κ' τῶν σύν αὐτοῦ λοιπῶν ἁγίων, ζήτ' σεπτεμβρίῳ κ´ – *13 (December) of the Holy Martyrs Eustratios and the rest of the saints together with him, see 20 September.*

In the perpendicular arch from east to west, two other martyrs are depicted:

– Ὁ Ἅγιος Τάραχος – St Tarachos;
– Ὁ Ἅγιος Ἀνδρόνικος – St Andronikos.

The feast day of both holy martyrs is celebrated by the Orthodox Church on 12 October. They are depicted richly garbed. It has been suggested that the appearance here of St Andronikos, a relatively obscure saint, can only be explained by his status as patron of the incumbent emperor in Metochites' time (Andronikos II), rather than because he belongs here according to any iconographic programme.[110] However, this is not the only possibility; there is a perfectly credible calendrical explanation. The selection of the saints in the narthexes and their feast days given aforementioned shows that they are related to the beginning of the Byzantine year in September and the autumn liturgy. For September, the *menologion* in cod. Dujčev Gr 177, f. 10 v records: ιβ´ τῶν ἁγίων μαρτύρων μαρτύρων Πρόβου, Ταράχου κ' Ἀνδρονίκου – *12 (October) Holy Martyrs Probus, Tarachos and Andronikos*. In other words, a service book had been in use in the Chora since the eleventh century in which the three saints are referred to as a group.

On the opposite arch, a pair of saints are also represented, with no surviving inscriptions. Based on the earlier logic regarding St Tarachos and St Andronikos, it may be assumed that these are Sts Marcianus and Martyrios (25 October) or Sts Plato and Romanus (17 November). These are all normally depicted as young and beardless, as here.[111]

3. *Christ taken to Jerusalem for Passover* – κ(αὶ) ἐπορεύοντο οἱ γονεῖς αὐτοῦ κατ' ἔτος εἰς Ἰ(ερουσα)λὴμ| τῇ ἑορτῇ τοῦ Πάσχα – *His parents went to Jerusalem every year at the Feast of the Passover* (Luke 2:41). Ἰ(ησοῦ)ς Χ

[109] Dionysius of Phourna, *Ἑρμηνεία*, p. 278. The Painter's manual of the priest Daniel is one of the sources of Dionysius, and appears in the *Appendices* of Papadopoulos-Kerameus' edition of Dionysius. My research shows that this text was created in Crete in the fifteenth century and was in use at the Balkans at least by the end of the sixteenth century. Moutafov, *Митрополитският*, pp. 291–292.

[110] Magdalino, 'Theodore Metochites', pp. 179–181; cf. Ousterhout, *Finding a Place*, p. 43. Neither of these authors pays attention to the fact that Sts Tarachos and Andronikos form a pair and dealing with them independently is untenable.

[111] Dionysius of Phourna, *Ἑρμηνεία*, p. 158.

(ριστὸ)ς is inscribed above Christ, and above the Theotokos traces of the letters Μή(τη)ρ Θ(εο)ῦ are discernible.

In the arch over the scene, the following are represented:

- Ὁ Ἅγιος Ἀνεμπόδιστος – St Anempodistos;
- Ὁ Ἅγιος Ἐλπιδηφόρος – St Elpidephoros;
- Ὁ Ἅγιος Ἀκίνδυνος – St Akindynos;
- Ὁ Ἅγιος Ἀφθόνιος – St Aphthonios;
- Ὁ Ἅγιος Πηγάσιος – St Pegasios.

All these saints are venerated on 2 November as Anargyroi ('Unmercenaries'). In Cod. Dujčev Gr 177, f. 11 r, this day is recorded as β΄ (νοεμβρίῳ) τῶν ἁγίων μαρτύρων Ἀκινδύνου κ' τῶν σύν αὐτοῦ, ζήτ' σεπτεμβρίῳ ιε΄ – *2 (November) of the Holy Martyr Akindynos and those with him, see 15 September.*

4. *The Nativity* – Ἡ Χ(ριστο)ῦ Γέννησις – *The Nativity of Christ.* A damaged inscription above the scene reads: μὴ φοβεῖσθε·| ἰδοὺ γὰρ εὐγγελίζομαι ὑμῖν χαρὰν| μεγάλην, ἥτης (sic! ἥτις) ἔσται παντὶ τῷ λαῷ ... – *Do not be afraid. I bring you good news that will cause great joy for all the people* (Luke 2:10).

   In the arch from north to south, above the *Nativity*, the following are depicted:

   - Ὁ Ἅγιος Φιλήμων – St Philemon;
   - Ὁ Ἅγιος Λεύκιος – St Leukios;
   - Ὁ Ἅγιος Ἀγαθόνικος – St Agathonikos;
   - Ὁ Ἅγιος Θύρσος – St Thyrsos;
   - Ὁ Ἅγιος Ἀπο|(λ)λώνιος – St Apollonios.

   With the exception of St Agathonikos, all the saints in this arch are venerated on 14 December. In all probability, St Agathapous should be present here, rather than St Agathonikos, if the group of saints is to correspond to the group described by the Priest Daniel.[112] The painter probably made this mistake because neither name is specifically mentioned in Cod. Dujčev Gr 177, f. 11 v, which records ιδ΄ (δεκεμβρίῳ) τῶν ἁγίων Θύρσου, Φιλήμονα κ' τῶν σύν αὐτῶν – *14 (December) of the Saints Thyrsos, Philemon, and those with them*, leading him to substitute Agathonikos for Agathopous.

5. *The Return of the Holy Family from Egypt* – ... χρηματισθεὶς δὲ κατ' ὄναρ ἀνεχώρησεν εἰς τὰ μέρη τῆς Γαλιλαίας, κ(αὶ) ἐλθὼν κατῴκησεν εἰς πόλιν λεγομένην Ναζαρέτ, ... – *And being warned by God in a dream, he turned aside into the region of Galilee. And he came and dwelt in a city called Nazareth* (Matt. 2:22–23).

6. *The Baptism of Christ* – no inscription survives. The scene illustrates Matt. 3:16, 17; Mark 1:9–11; Luke 3:21.

[112] Ibidem, p. 272.

7. *The Temptation of Christ* – this comprises five scenes, as follows; Christ is indicated in each with the inscription Ἰ(ησοῦ)ς Χ(ριστὸ)ς:
   (a) *The Devil tells Christ to Turn the Stones into Bread*: Εἰ υἱὸς εἶ τοῦ Θ (εο)ῦ, εἰπὲ| ἵνα οἱ λίθοι οὗτοι| ἄρτοι γένωνται – *If thou be the Son of God, command that these stones be made bread* (Matt. 4:3); and Christ's answer: γέγραπται, οὐκ ἐπ' ἄρτ(ῳ)| μόνῳ ζήσεται ἄν(θρωπ) ος, ἀλλ' ἐπὶ| παντὶ ῥήματι ἐκπορευο|μένῳ διὰ στόματος Θ(εο)ῦ – *It is written, Man shall not live by bread alone, but by every word that proceedeth out of the mouth of God* (Matt. 4:4).
   (b) *The Devil Promises Christ the Kingdoms of the World*: Ταῦτα πάντα σοι| δώσω, ἐὰν πεσὼν| προσκυνήσῃς μοι – *All these things will I give thee, if thou wilt fall down and worship me* (Matt. 4:9); and Christ's answer: ὕπαγε ὀπίσω μου|, σατανᾶ· (γέγραπται γάρ, Κύριον τὸν Θεόν σου προσκυνήσεις καὶ αὐτῷ μόνῳ λατρεύσεις) – *Get thee hence, Satan: for it is written, Thou shalt worship the Lord thy God, and him only shalt thou serve* (Matt. 4:10; Luke 4:8).
   (c) *The Devil Takes Christ to Jerusalem*: Τότε παραλαμβάνει αὐτὸν ὁ διάβολος εἰς τ(ὴν) ἁγίαν πόλιν, (καὶ ἵστησιν αὐτὸν ἐπὶ τὸ πτερύγιον τοῦ ἱεροῦ) – *Then the devil taketh him up into the holy city, and setteth him on a pinnacle of the temple* (Matt. 4:5).
   (d) *The Devil Tells Christ to Cast Himself from the Pinnacle of the Temple*: εἰ υἱὸς εἶ τοῦ Θ(εο)ῦ,| βάλε σεαυτόν κάτω· – *If thou be the Son of God, cast thyself down* (Matt. 4:6); and Christ's answer: <πάλιν> γέγραπται, οὐκ ἐκπειρά|σεις Κύριον τὸν Θ(εό)ν σου – *It is written again, Thou shalt not tempt the Lord thy God* (Matt. 4:7).
   (e) *John the Forerunner Bearing Witness to Christ*. Around a group of men conversing with John (<Ὁ Ἅγιος> Ἰω(άννης) ὁ Πρ(ό)δ(ρο)μος – *St John the Forerunner*), is written: οὗτος ἦν ὃν εἶπον, ὁ ὀπίσω μου| ἐρχόμενος ἔμπροσθέν μου γέγονεν,| ὅτι πρῶτός μου ἦν – *This was he of whom I spake, He that cometh after me is preferred before me: for he was before me* (John 1:15).

   In the arch, below the *Temptation of Christ*, the following are depicted:
   – Ὁ Ἅγιος Βικέντιος – St Vicentius. His *orarion* (deacon's stole) is inscribed: ἅγιος;
   – Ὁ Ἅγιος Βίκτωρ – St Victor;
   – Ὁ Ἅγιος Μηνᾶς – St Menas;
   – Ὁ Ἅγιος Φλῶρος – St Floros;
   – Ὁ Ἅγιος Λαῦρος – St Lauros.

Sts Vicentius, Victor, and Menas are venerated together on 11 November, while Sts Floros and Lauros are venerated on 18 August. With the latter paired saints, there apparently is a departure from the feasts of the saints celebrated in the autumn/winter cycle, which will be commented later. In cod. Dujčev Gr 177, f. 13 v, the entire *menologion* ends in August with Sts Floros and Lauros: ιη′ (αὐγούστου) τῶν ἁγίων μαρτύρων μαρτύρων Φλώρου και Λαῦρου – *18 (August) Holy Martyrs Floros and Lauros*. Their appearance together with saints venerated in November is also due to the manuscript, which specifies: ζήτ' ὀκτωβρίῳ εἰς ι′: 2(?) – *see 10 October: 2*. The latter specification, however, refers to 10 October in the *menologion*, clarifying which passages of the Gospel should be read on a particular day. In the case of f. 10 v, it is noted that on this day Sts Eulampius and Eulampia are venerated: ι′ (ὀκτωμβρίῳ) τῶν ἁγίων μαρτύρων μαρτύρων Εὐλαμπίου καὶ Εὐλαμπίας – *10 October, Holy Martyrs Eulampios and Eulampia*. There follow instructions for the passages in Mark to be read on this particular day.

8. (a) *The Marriage at Cana* – no surviving inscriptions.[113] *The Marriage at Cana* and the *Multiplication of the Loaves* are both divided into two scenes, with Christ as the main figure in each. The result is four compositional schemes centred around the themes of wine and bread. Set on the main axis of the church, *The Marriage at Cana* and *The Multiplication of Loaves* are given special prominence, because the wine and bread refer to sacrament of Eucharist, but sometimes are just wine and bread when outside the bema, which probably means that the outer narthex was used as a refectory.[114]

   Although the central image of the mosaic in the third vault is missing, significant parts are preserved. The main scene of banqueting has been lost, but the table legs are visible in the north-west corner, and a detail of a white bullock being slain for the feast. Also in the corner is the miracle of the transformation of water into wine, where men fill big pithoi with water. There the mosaic jars are made by terracotta tesserae or pieces of real ceramic vessels. Some scholars unite these two episodes, which is correct, but here I follow my own division of the scenes.

   (b) *The Transformation of Water into Wine* – no surviving inscriptions. The scene illustrates John 2:1–10.

9. (a) *The Multiplication of Loaves* – no surviving inscriptions.

[113] In *The Marriage at Cana*, Van Millingen noticed an Arabic numeral above the entrance, which he interpreted as a date, corresponding to 1302/1303, suggesting this was when Metochites' reconstruction began: see Van Millingen, *Byzantine Churches*, p. 300. Epigraphically and historically, this is questionable; in contemporary Byzantine studies, the reconstruction is understood to have been carried out c. 1315–1321, as mentioned earlier: see Kuniholm and Striker, 'Dendrochronological', p. 395, fig. 2. For the period 1313–1317, see Smyrlis, 'Contextualizing', pp. 69–111.

[114] Moutafov, *Богородица*, p. 87.

(b) *The Multiplication of Loaves* (the twelve baskets) – no surviving inscriptions.

10. *The Three Magi Before King Herod* – κ(α)ὶ ἰδοὺ μάγ(οι) ἀπὸ ἀνατολ(ῶν) παρεγένοντ(ο)| εἰς Ἰ(εροσό)λυμ(α) λέγοντ(ες·) ποῦ ἐστιν ὁ τεχθεὶς| βασιλεὺς τῶν Ἰουδαίων – . . . *behold, there came wise men from the east to Jerusalem, saying, where is he that is born King of the Jews?* (Matt. 2:1–2).

    In this scene, in an arch, the following three saints are represented:
    - Ὁ Ἅγιος Ἄβιβος – St Abibos;
    - Ὁ Ἅγιος Γουρίας – St Gourias;
    - Ὁ Ἅγιος Σαμωνᾶς – St Samonas.

    All three are venerated on 15 November. Cod. Dujčev Gr 177, f. 11 v records: ιε΄ (νοεμβρίῳ) των ἁγίων ὁμολ(ογητῶν), ζήτ' ὀκτωβρίῶ κε΄ – *15 November of the Holy Confessors, see 25 October*. The saints are not mentioned by name in the manuscript, as they were both martyrs and confessors. For 25 October, Cod. Dujčev Gr 177, f. 11 r gives Sts Martyrios and Marcian (see III.2) – κε΄ (ὀκτωβρίῳ) τῶν ἁγίων νοταρίων Μαρκιανοῦ καὶ Μαρτυρίου – *25 October, Sts Martyrios and Marcian, the Notaries*.

11. *Christ Healing a Man with Dropsy* – Ὁ Χ(ριστὸ)ς ἰώμ(ενός) τ(ὸν) ὑδρωπηκ(όν) (sic! ὑδρωπικόν) (Luke 14:2–4).

12. *The Flight of Elizabeth and John* – Ἡ Φηγὴ (sic! Φυγὴ) τ(ῆς) Ἐλισάβετ – *The Flight of Elizabeth*.

    Over the *Flight of Elizabeth* in the arch, the following martyrs are depicted:
    - Ὁ Ἅγιος Ἔγγραφος (sic! Εὔγραφος) – St Eugraphos;
    - Ὁ Ἅγιος Μηνᾶς – St Menas;
    - Ὁ Ἅγιος Ἑρμογένης – St Hermogenes.

    Sts Eugraphos and Hermogenes are normally venerated on 10 December along with St Menas Kallikelados. However, the surname 'Kallikelados' is omitted here, in line with the wording of the *menologion* in the Dujčev manuscript. Another 'mistake' that also corresponds to the manuscript is in the name of the first saint: Ἅγιος Εὔγραφος ('good scribe') is spelled here as Ἅγιος Ἔγγραφος, which means 'entered' (that is, 'written in', 'registered'). There is no such Orthodox saint and this identification or even joke is probably related to the *Enrolment for Taxation* (III.2, see Figure 13), which required registration (ἐγγραφή). This registration, which is in fact taxation, was probably intended to show that even the painters were Metochites' taxpayers, and this deliberate term could be also deemed to be the artist's indictment of the *ktetor*'s mercenary nature and sins in his capacity as the collector of taxes even from saints. The entry in Cod.

Figure 13 Enrolment for taxation, fourteenth-century mosaic in the outer narthex of the Chora. Photo: Author

Dujčev Gr 177, f. 11 v, records: ι΄ (μηνί δεκεμβρίω) τῶν ἁγίων μαρτύρων μαρτύρων Μηνᾶ, Ἑρμογένη κ' Ἐγγράφου – *10 December of the holy martyrs Menas, Hermogenes, and Engraphos.*

13. *Herod Inquiring of the Priests and Scribes* – no surviving inscriptions.
14. *Herod Orders the Massacre of the Innocent in Bethlehem* – Τότε Ἡρῴδης ἰδ(ὼν) ὅτι ἐνεπαίχθη ὑπὸ τ(ῶν) μάγων, ἐθυμώθ[η]| λίαν, κ(αὶ) ἀποστείλας ἀνεῖλε πάντ(ας) τοὺς παῖδας τοὺς ἐν Βηθλεὲμ,| κ(αὶ) ἐν πᾶσι τοῖς ὁρίοις αὐτῆς ἀπὸ διετοῦς κ(α)ὶ κατωτέρω – *Then Herod, when he saw that he was mocked of the wise men, was exceeding wroth, and sent forth, and slew all the children that were in Bethlehem, and in all the coasts thereof, from two years old and under* (Matt. 2:16).
15. *Mothers Mourning Their Children* – [Φωνὴ ἐν Ῥαμᾷ] ἠκούσθη, θρῆνος κ(αὶ) κλαυθμὸς κ(αὶ) ὀδυρμὸς πολύς· – *A voice was heard in Ramah, lamentation, weeping, and great mourning, . . .* (Matt. 2:18).
16. *The Samaritan Woman* – Ὁ Χ(ριστὸ)ς διαλεγόμενος τῇ Σαμαρείτ[ιδι] – *Christ talking to a Samaritan woman* (John 4:7).
17. *Christ Heals the Paralytic in the Pool of Bethesda* – κλίνης ἔγειρε τὸν παράλυτον λόγ[ω] as a periphrasis for: λέγει αὐτῷ ὁ Ἰησοῦς· ἔγειρε, ἆρον τὸν κράβαττόν σου καὶ περιπάτει – *Rise, take up thy bed, and walk* (John 5:8).
18. (a) *The Massacre of the Innocents* – no extant inscriptions. The scene illustrates Matt. 2:16–18.

    (b) *The Massacre of the Innocents* (continuation) – no extant inscriptions.

19. *Christ Healing the Paralytic at Capernaum* – Ὁ Χ(ριστὸ)ς λέγων (sic! Λέγει) τῷ παραλυτικῷ· (τέκνον,) ἀφέωνταί| (σοι) αἱ ἁμαρτίαις (sic! ἁμαρτίαι) σου – *Jesus . . . said to the paralyzed man, (Son,) your sins are forgiven* (Mark 2:5).
20. *Flight into Egypt* – Ἡ πρὸς τὴν Αἴγυπτον φυγὴ (Matt. 2:13,14).
    In the south-east bay of the exonarthex:
    – [Ὁ Ἅγιος] Εὐθύ[μιος] – St Euthymios the Great.
21. *Christ Calling Zacchaeus* – no extant inscriptions.
22. *The Return of the Magi to the East* – no extant inscriptions.

Tombs (E–Z – Figure 7)

There are four burial recesses in the outer narthex, of which Tomb E will be commented on in connection with the *parekklesion*.

Of Tomb G, only a fragment of the murals survives, featuring the patron standing before the enthroned Virgin and Child. Researchers assume that this was the last burial before the fall of Constantinople to the Ottomans in 1453. Painting here is exceptionally soft, gradations of the colour create smooth transitions, no rough lines are witnessed, patches of colour are used to give the work depth, that is, everything is reminiscent of Giotto's touch and a Renaissance of an Italian type.[115]

IV. *Parekklesion* (south chapel) (see Figure 9)

The frescoes of the *parekklesion*, built by Theodore Metochites, were created at the same time as the mosaics of the church.[116] Two themes dominate. One relates to its role as funerary chapel,[117] leading to a focus on Resurrection and Judgement expressed most clearly in the monumental *Anastasis* (Resurrection) and *Last Judgement* scenes. The other is a focus on the Virgin, with a full-length depiction of her as the Virgin *Eleousa*, a series of scenes from the Old Testament traditionally understood to prefigure her, and the appearance of the four Melodist saints.

1. The Church Fathers on the Apse Wall
    Represented in the altar conch are:
    – ὁ Ἅγ(ιος) Ἰω(άννης) ὁ Χρ(υσ)ό(σ)τ(ομος) – St John Chrysostom;
    – ὁ Ἅγ(ιος) Βασίλειος (ὁ Μέγας) – St Basil the Great;
    – ὁ Ἅγ(ιος) Γρηγόριος ὁ Θεολόγος – St Gregory the Theologian;
    – ὁ Ἅγ(ιος) Κύριλλος (Ἀλεξανδρείας) – St Cyril of Alexandria.

[115] Underwood, *The Kariye*, III, p. 549. See also the insightful recent analysis in Bacci, 'Tomb G', pp. 100–134.
[116] Underwood, *The Kariye*, I, pp. 187–309; Underwood, *The Kariye*, III, photos 335–553.
[117] Der Nersessian, 'Program', pp. 303–350.

These appear in their liturgical garments, strengthening the symbolism of the Eucharist, appropriate for this area of the chapel.[118]

2. *The Resurrection* (Anastasis) – Ἡ Ἀνάστασις (τοῦ Χριστοῦ) = Ἡ εἰς Ἅδην κάθοδος τοῦ Κυρίου – *The Descent of the Lord into Hades.*

   The *Anastasis* in the eastern bay of the *parekklesion* is based on the apocryphal Gospel of Nikodemos and is the usual Byzantine representation of Christ's Resurrection.[119] As Adam and Eve are raised out of their tombs by the hands of the resurrected Son of God (Ἰ(ησοῦ)ς Χ(ριστὸ)ς), the guarantee of salvation is held out to those buried in the sarcophagi below. These connotations across temporal barriers are emphasised both in the funeral service and in the composition of the murals.[120] It is worth noting that in the *Anastasis*, Christ's right hand gestures both toward Adam, whom he raises from the dead, and toward the *diakonikon*, which in Metochites' days had already been incorporated into the chapel[121] (see Figure 14).

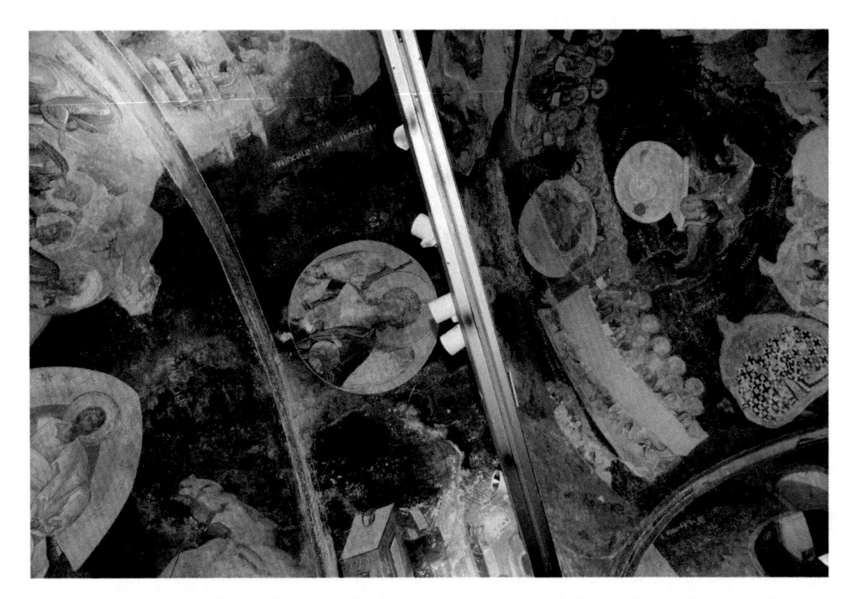

Figure 14 View of the ceiling of the east part of the funeral chapel (*parekklesion*) of the Chora. Photo: Author

[118] Underwood, *The Kariye*, IV, plans 202, 203 (Resurrection scenes), and 243–248 (symbolism of the Eucharist).

[119] Underwood, *The Kariye*, I, pp. 192–195; Der Nersessian, 'Program', pp. 320–322.

[120] Ousterhout, 'Temporal', p. 74.

[121] Ousterhout, *Finding a Place*, p. 18, plan 8.

3. *The Archangel Michael* – Ὁ Ἄ(ρχων) Μιχ(αὴλ). Michael is holding a sphere inscribed: Χ Δ Κ – Χ(ριστὸς) Δ(ίκαιος) Κ(ριτής) – *Christ the Just Judge.*

Another example of the use of the cryptogram Χ Δ Κ is witnessed on an icon also representing Michael the Archangel, from the second half of the fourteenth century, now kept at the Byzantine and Christian Museum, Athens.[122] The Archangel is rendered bust-length, holding a spear in his right hand and the *akakia* (orb) in his left hand with Χ Δ Κ inscribed on it.

The orb in Michael's hand is a symbol of his patronage of the Byzantine emperor and his secular power. The acronym, combining Michael's name with two of the most important popular attributes of Christ ('just' and 'judge'), can be associated with the role of Michael the Archangel as psychopomp ('guide of souls') and judge of souls on behalf of the Saviour at the Last Judgement (see Figure 15). The fact that the orb is ethereal, that

Figure 15 Archangel Michael, fourteenth-century icon from Constantinople, Byzantine and Christian Museum, Athens. Photo credit: Byzantine and Christian Museum, Athens

[122] *Το Βυζάντιο*, p. 56, fig. 11.

is, the folds of his mantle are seen through it, suggesting that the globe is not a model of the earth or of secular power, but rather of Heaven and Paradise, gives me grounds for such an assumption.

4. *The Raising of the Widow's Son* – ὁ Χ(ριστὸ)ς ἀνιστὰ[ς (ἀνιστῶν?) τὸ]ν [υἱὸ]ν τῆς χήρας – *Christ raising the widow's son*. This scene illustrates Luke 7:12–15.
5. *The Raising of the Daughter of Jairus* – no extant inscriptions.

Christ Rising the Widow's Son and *Christ Rising the Daughter of Jairus* complete the cycle of Ministry and Miracles of Christ that began in the narthexes.[123] The emotion of the scenes is similarly emphasised by the diagonals, and the message of both is heightened by the compositional parallels with the *Anastasis*. Both raisings from the dead from the New and the Old Testament act as a preparation for the resurrection of the dead at the end of time, depicted in the vault above.[124]

6. *The Last Judgement* – Ἡ Δευτέρα τοῦ Χ(ριστο)ῦ παρουσία.

The scenes from the Biblical past at the east end of the chapel act as a preparation for the events of the future or for the *Last Judgement*,[125] which is represented in the vault of the east bay. This exceptional representation follows earlier models, but the scene was normally organised in registers on a flat surface.[126] At the Chora, the placement of the *Last Judgment* in a domical vault is unique and provides an iconographical unity and thus a heightened importance lacking in all other versions (Torcello, icon from Mount Sinai), and has an emphasis on the future.[127] The only other example of a *Last Judgment* set into a dome appears in the narthex of the Panagia Phorbiotissa in the village of Asinou, Cyprus, from the 1330s.[128] The most striking detail of the composition in my view is the so-called Scroll of Heaven, signalling the end of days with the sun, moon, and stars, which is usually attributed to Theodore Metochites' astronomical studies.[129]

The *Last Judgment* features groups (choirs) of saints:

- Χορὸς ἱεράρχων – the Choir of the Hierarchs;
- Χορὸς ὁσίων – the Choir of the Blessed;
- Χορὸς γυναικῶν – the Choir of the Holy Women;
- Χορὸς μαρτύρων – the Choir of the Martyrs.

Next to the righteous in the *Last Judgment* is inscribed:

---

[123] Underwood, *The Kariye*, I, pp. 196–199; Der Nersessian, 'Program', pp. 322–324.
[124] Ousterhout, 'Temporal', p. 72. [125] Ibidem, p. 70. [126] Ibidem, p. 72.
[127] Ibidem, p. 72.
[128] Seymer et al., 'The Church of Asinou', pp. 336–340; Ousterhout, 'Temporal', p. 72.
[129] Bydén, *Theodore Metochites*; Ousterhout, *Finding a Place*, p. 65.

> (δεῦτε οἱ εὐλογημένοι τοῦ πατρός) μου,| [κληρον]ομήσατε τὴν ἡτοιμασμέν (ην)| ὑμῖν βασιλείαν ἀπὸ κατα|βολῆς κόσμου – *(Come, ye blessed of) my Father, inherit the kingdom prepared for you from the foundation of the world* (Matt. 25:34).

Next to the sinners is inscribed:

> πορε[ύ]εσ[θε ἀπ' ἐμοῦ οἱ] κατηραμένοι εἰς τὸ πῦρ τὸ αἰώνιον τὸ ἡτοιμασμ (ένον) τῷ διαβόλῳ| κ(αὶ) τοῖς ἀγγέλοις αὐτοῦ – *Depart from me, ye cursed, into everlasting fire, prepared for the devil and his angels* (Matt. 25:41).

7. The *Virgin Eleousa* with the following inscriptions: Μή(τη)ρ Θ(εο)ῦ/ Ἰ(ησοῦ)ς Χ(ριστὸ)ς – *Mother of God/ Jesus Christ*.

   This full-length depiction of Mary, her hands gently pulling the Christ child toward her cheek, has been characterised as 'one of the most moving types of the Eleousa (Tenderness) in Byzantine art'.[130] The Virgin Eleousa here is not as conservative and calm as the Virgin Hodegetria on the templon of the *naos*, probably because the mosaics in the *naos* replicate those of the twelfth century.[131] This is, of course, also due to the different techniques, as painting offers wider opportunities for expressiveness.
8. *The Entry of the Elect into Paradise* – no surviving inscriptions. This is the last episode of the *Last Judgment* composition. The scene is divided vertically into two halves by the centrally positioned Gates of Eden, guarded by a cherub with folded wings wearing a red cloak. A group of various figures on the left represents the different categories of the elect, led by St Peter, who puts his key into the lock of the gates. The upper cornice of the symbolic gates to Eden resembles marble and is three-pitched, narrowing downwards; the gates have a sill and two doorsteps. This painted gate is strongly reminiscent of the marble frame of the entryway that leads to the *diakonikon* next to the chapel. On the left is Eden, where light and lush verdure abound. The Penitent Thief, wearing nothing but a loincloth and holding a cross, meets those chosen for salvation. He points to the Theotokos sitting on a throne as the Queen of Heavens, surrounded by angels.

   This scene is of paramount importance to understanding the Chora, for there are at least four figures in the foreground whose identification would be of much help to researchers. Unfortunately, their heads are completely lost. In any event, however, it is noteworthy that St Peter and the next two men are barefoot, while the figure behind them wears red boots. The character above them wears a purple himation (a type of cloak) and a green mantle bordered with a gold trim. Behind this figure stands what appears to be a patriarch,

[130] Lazarev, *История*, p. 161. [131] Ousterhout, *Finding a Place*, p. 51.

followed by a man in monk's habit, and, finally, a man in aristocratic garb. It is not unlikely that here were represented the emperor, the patriarch, the hegoumenos of the monastery, and several noblemen associated with the Chora.

9. *The Bearing of the Ark of the Covenant* – . . . ὡς συνετέλεσε Σαλωμ(ὼν) τοῦ οἰκοδομῆσα[ι τὸν ο]ἶκον Κυρίου| <καὶ τὸν οἶκον αὐτοῦ μετὰ εἴκοσιν ἔτη, τότε> [ἐ]ξεκκλησίασεν <ὁ βασιλεὺς Σαλωμὼν> πάντας τοὺς πρεσβυτέρους Ἰ(σρα)ὴλ ἐν Σιὼν τοῦ ἀνενεγκ[εῖν]| τὴν κιβωτ(ὸν) διαθήκ(ης) Κ(υρίο)υ ἐκ πόλ(εως) Δα(υὶδ) αὕτη ἐ[στὶ Σ]ιὼν| <ἐν μηνὶ Ἀθανίν. Καὶ ἦραν> οἱ ἱερεῖς τ(ὴν) κιβω(τὸν) τῆς διαθήκης Κ(υρίο)υ κ(αὶ) τὸ σκή|νωμα τοῦ μαρτυρίου <καὶ τὰ σκεύη τὰ ἅγια τὰ ἐν τῷ σκηνώματι τοῦ μαρτυρίου, . . . > – *Now Solomon assembled the elders of Israel and all the heads of the tribes, the chief fathers of the children of Israel, to King Solomon in Jerusalem, that they might bring up the ark of the covenant of the Lord from the City of David, which is Zion. Therefore all the men of Israel assembled with King Solomon at the feast in the month of Ethanim, which is the seventh month. So all the elders of Israel came, and the priests took up the ark. Then they brought up the ark of the Lord, the tabernacle of meeting, and all the holy furnishings that were in the tabernacle* (somewhat abridged with fewer additions after 3 Kings 8:1–4)

   Both the *Bearing of the Ark of the Covenant* and the *Installation of the Ark in the Holy of Holies* prefigure the *Presentation of the Virgin in the Temple*, found in the inner narthex of the Chora.[132]

10. *The Land and Sea Giving Up Their Dead* – no extant inscriptions.
11. *An Angel and a Soul* – no extant inscriptions. This probably illustrates Luke 12:19–21: *And I will say to my soul, Soul, thou hast much goods laid up for many years; take thine ease, eat, drink, and be merry. But God said unto him, Thou fool, this night thy soul shall be required of thee: then whose shall those things be, which thou hast provided? So is he that layeth up treasure for himself, and is not rich toward God*. This is the parable of the rich man, who hoarded wealth for himself, but did not endow God/the Church with his riches. In this connection, I deem it highly improbable that the sinner's soul should be identified with Metochites. Quite the contrary; this scene refers to all rich men who failed to endow churches like the Chora with their fortune.
12. *The Virgin with the Child with Angels* – in the centre of the dome, there is a medallion inscribed: Μή(τη)ρ Θ(εο)ῦ – *Mother of God*, while in the folds of the dome, over each angel is inscribed: Ἄγγελ(ος) Κ(υρίο)υ – *Angel of God* (see Figure 16).
13. *The Four Hymnographers*:
   In the north-east domical pendentive with the Theotokos:

[132] Underwood, *The Kariye*, II, plans 119–128; Ousterhout, 'Temporal', p. 71.

Figure 16 Virgin Mary with Child and angels, dome of the funeral chapel (*parekklesion*) of the Chora. Photo: Author

- ὁ Ἅγ(ιος) Ἰω(άννης) ὁ Δαμασκηνός – St John of Damascus (4 December) holds a scroll inscribed: <τὸν> πρ(ὸ αἰώνιων ἐκ πατρὸς γεννηθέντα, . . . ?) – *he who was born of the father before all time*. . . . Until now the Damascene was believed to be holding a scroll inscribed: ποία τοῦ| βίου τρυ|φ[ὴ δι] αμένει| λύπ[ης] <ἀμέτοχος> – *What joy of life remains without its share of sorrow* (opening words of his Idiomela for the Funeral Service), an interpretation that cannot be sustained.[133]

In the south-east domical pendentive:

- St Cosmas the Hymnographer – ὁ Ἅγ(ιος) Κοσμᾶς ὁ ποιητής – St Cosmas the Poet (14 October). I would not venture to offer a reading of this scroll, but by analogy with the other inscriptions of the hymnographers, I would suggest: Εἰκών ἀπαράλλακτε τοῦ ὄντος ἀκίνητε, σφραγίς ἀναλλοίωτε, υἱὲ λόγε σοφία καὶ βραχίων δεξιὰ ὑψίστου σθένους . . .[134] – *An image like a motionless being, an unalterable seal; O son, the word, wisdom and*

[133] Der Nersessian, 'Program', p. 310. [134] Dionysius of Phourna, *Ἑρμηνεία*, p. 220.

strength of the right hand of the most high, we glorify thee with thy father and the spirit.[135]

In the south-west domical pendentive:

- St Joseph the Hymnographer – ὁ Ἅγ(ιος) Ἰωσὴφ ὁ ποιητής – St Joseph the Poet (3 April) holds a scroll that I would suggest reads: <οὐρανὸν ὁ τανύσας βουλήματι οὐρανὸν ἐπίγειον> ἄλλον ἐπλάτυνε σέ, θεομῆτορ ἄχραντε, καὶ ἐκ σοῦ ἀνα(τείλας ἐπέφανε?) – *o spotless mother of God, thou has stretched out the heavens at thine own will and laid out the earth as another heaven, and hast shown it in what has risen from thee.*[136] On this scroll, the only word that is certain is ἄχραντε, and the reading Ἱλαστήρι|ον τοῦ κόσ|μου χαῖρε,| ἄχραντε| Δέσποινα . . . – *Propitiation of the world, hail, spotless Virgin*[137] has previously been offered; a reading I disagree with.

In the north-west domical pendentive:

- ὁ Ἅγ(ιος) Θεοφάνης (ὁ Γραπτός) – St Theophanes (Graptos) (11 October). I would not venture to offer a reading of this scroll. It has been interpreted as containing the words: Εἰς γῆν| ἀπεστρά(φημεν)| παρα|βάτες| (τοῦ) Θ(εο)ῦ <τὴν ἐντολὴν τὴν ἔνθεον> – *We were turned back to earth after having transgressed God's divine commandment* (sixth Ode of Theophanes' Canon for the Funeral Service).[138]

For the reconstruction of these inscriptions, I have used the description by Dionysius of Phourna of the hymnographers in the domical pendentives in a narthex with the Theotokos in its centre. This, along with other descriptions contained in the eighteenth-century *Hermeneiai*, is apparently based on earlier texts or depicts particular Byzantine churches.[139]

It would be more usual to represent the four evangelists around the image of Christ. In this case, however, there are probably two reasons why they are replaced by the four Melodist saints, corresponding to the two main themes of the decoration of the *parekklesion*. First, they wrote hymns honouring the Theotokos, connecting with the focus on Mary;[140] and second, their hymns were incorporated into the funeral service as an expression of salvation, connecting with the role of the *parekklesion* as funeral chapel.[141]

Among the extant individual representations in the chapel, there is also a fragment in the west area of the chamber inscribed: δίκα[ι]ος Μελχισεδὲκ – the righteous Melchizedek.

14. *Jacob's Ladder* and *Jacob Wrestling with the Angel*:

---

[135] As translated by Hetherington, *The Painter's Manual*, p. 85. [136] Ibidem.

[137] Underwood, *The Kariye*, I, p. 217. [138] Ibidem.

[139] See Περὶ νάρθηκος in Dionysius of Phourna, *Ἑρμηνεία*, p. 220.

[140] Underwood, *The Kariye*, I, pp. 217–222. [141] Ousterhout, 'Temporal', p. 71.

(a) καὶ ἔλαβ(εν) <Ἰακὼβ>| ἀπὸ τῶν λίθ(ων) τοῦ τόπου, κ(αὶ) ἔ|θηκε πρ(ὸς) κε|φαλῆ(ς) αὐτοῦ| κ(αὶ) ἐκοιμήθη| ἐν τῷ τόπῳ ἐκείνῳ|κ(αὶ) ἐνυπνιάσθη, . . . – . . . *and he (Jacob) took of the stones of that place, and put them for his pillows, and lay down in that place to sleep. And he dreamed, . . .* (Genesis 28:11–12);

(b) . . . κ(αὶ) ἰδοὺ κλίμαξ ἐστηριγμένη ἐν| τῇ γῇ, ἧς ἡ κεφαλὴ ἀφικ[νεῖ]το εἰς τ(ὸν) οὐρανόν,| κ(αὶ) οἱ ἄγγελοι τοῦ Θ(εο)ῦ ἀνέβαιν(ον) καὶ κατέβαιν(ον)| ἐπ᾽ αὐτῆν ὁ δὲ Κ(ύριο)ς ἐπεστήρι|κτο ἐπ᾽ αὐτῆς – . . . *and behold a ladder set up on the earth, and the top of it reached to heaven: and behold the angels of God ascending and descending on it* (Genesis 28:12).

15. *Moses and the Burning Bush*:

(a) + καὶ εἰσῆλθε (sic! ἦλθεν)| εἰς τὸ ὄρος τοῦ Θ(εο)ῦ Χωρήβ.| ὤφθη δὲ αὐτῷ ἄγγελος Κ(υρίο)υ ἐν φλογὶ| πυρός (sic! Πυρὶ φλογὸς) ἐκ τοῦ βάτου, . . . – *Now Moses (was tending the flock of Jethro his father-in-law, the priest of Midian, and he led the flock to the far side of the wilderness and) came to Horeb, the mountain of God. There the angel of the Lord appeared to him in flames of fire from within a bush* (somewhat abridged with changes Exodus 3:1–2).

(b) λῦσ(αι) τὸ ὑπόδημα| ἐκ τ(ῶν) ποδῶν σου· ὁ <γὰρ> τόπ(ος), ἐν [ᾧ σὺ ἕστηκα]ς,| [γῆ ἁγία ἐστί] – *put off thy shoes from off thy feet, for the place whereon thou standest is holy ground* (Exodus 3:5).

16. *Moses Hides his Face* – . . . ἀπέστρεψε δὲ Μω(υσῆ)ε (sic! Μωϋσῆς) τὸ πρόσωπο(ν) αὐτοῦ· εὐλαβεῖτο γὰρ κατεμ|βλέψαι ἐνώπιον τοῦ Θ(εο)ῦ – *(At this,) Moses hid his face, because he was afraid to look at God* (Exodus 3:6).

17. *The Bearing of the Sacred Vessels* – no extant inscriptions. The scenes *Bearing of the Ark of the Covenant*, *Bearing of the Sacred Vessels*, and the *Dedication of Solomon's Temple* belong to the same narrative, which culminates in the *Dedication of Solomon's Temple*. This detailed cycle has no parallel in other Byzantine churches, and only a few of the episodes appear in contemporary and later monuments.[142]

18. *The Dedication of Solomon's Temple* – κ(αὶ) ὁ βασιλεὺς κ(αὶ) πᾶς Ἰ(σρα)ὴλ ἔμπροσθ(εν) τῆς κιβωτοῦ . . . – *Also King Solomon, and all the congregation of Israel who were assembled with him, were with him before the ark, . . .* (3 Kings 8:5).

19. *The Installation of the Ark in the Holy of Holies* – κ(αὶ) εἰσφέρουσιν οἱ ἱερεῖς τὴν κιβωτ(ὸν) τῆς διαθήκης| εἰς τ(ὸν) τόπον αὐτῆς εἰς τὸ δαβὴρ (sic!

[142] Der Nersessian, 'Program', p. 338.

Δαβὶρ) τοῦ οἴκου, εἰς τὰ ἅγια| τ(ῶν) ἁγίων ὑπὸ τ(ὰς) πτέρυγας τῶν Χερουβίν (sic! Χερουβίμ·) – *Then the priests brought in the ark of the covenant of the Lord to its place, into the inner sanctuary of the temple, to the Most Holy Place, under the wings of the cherubim* (3 Kings 8: 6).

20. *Aaron and his Sons Before the Altar* – no extant inscriptions. The scene illustrates Ezekiel 43:27 (*When these days are over it shall be, on the eighth day and thereafter, that the priests shall offer your burnt offerings and your peace offerings on the altar; and I will accept you,' says the Lord God*) or Ezekiel 44:2–3 (*Then said the Lord unto me; This gate shall be shut, it shall not be opened, and no man shall enter in by it; because the Lord, the God of Israel, hath entered in by it, therefore it shall be shut. It is for the prince; the prince, he shall sit in it to eat bread before the Lord; he shall enter by the way of the porch of that gate, and shall go out by the way of the same*).
21. *The Prophecy of Isaiah* and *Angel Smiting the Assyrians before Jerusalem* – no extant inscriptions. The composition represents the destruction of the armies of Sennacherib, king of Assysia, prophesised by Isaiah to Hezekiah (Isa. 37:21–36; IV Kings 19:20–35).
22. *Martyrs and Warrior Saints*:

    In the bottom register of the chapel's south wall, in its east area, the following are represented in medallions:

    – ὁ Ἅγι(ος) Σέργιος – St Sergius;
    – ὁ Ἅγι(ος) Βάκχος – St Bacchus.

    The feast day of both falls on 7 October. The pair are patrons of an important Constantinopolitan church, the Church of Sts Sergius and Bacchus in Hormisdas (Hormisdas was a palace in the earlier Byzantine period), Ἐκκλησία τῶν Ἁγίων Σεργίου καὶ Βάκχου ἐν τοῖς Ὁρμίσδου, or Little Hagia Sophia. Their presence in the iconographic programme makes yet another association with a significant Constantinopolitan cult and the monument dedicated to it. The two saints are, of course, also found in the *menologion* in Cod. Dujčev Gr 177, f. 10 v.

    In the west area of the chapel's north wall, in the lower horizontal register, the following are depicted:

    – ὁ Ἅγι(ος) Σαμωνᾶς – St Samonas;
    – ὁ Ἅγι(ος) [Γουρίας?] – St Gourias.

    Sts Samonas and Gourias are paired together and venerated by the Orthodox Church on 15 November. It is, however, also the feast day of Hieromartyr Abibus (Ἄβιβος), meaning that the proposed identification here with St Gourias is not certain. At all events, here we have martyrs represented, continuing the series of such personages in the outer narthex.

On the north wall of the chapel's narthex, the following is depicted:

– ὁ Ἅγι(ος) Εὐστάθιος (ὁ Πλακίδας) – St Eustathios Plakidas (20 September).

In the east area of the chapel, on the west wall, the following is depicted:

– ὁ Ἅγι(ος) Γεώργιος – St George (23 April).

In the east area of the chapel, on the south wall, the following are depicted in medallions:

– ὁ Ἅγι(ος) Φλῶρος – St Floros;
– ὁ Ἅγι(ος) Λαῦρος – St Lauros.

As mentioned earlier, the feast day of the twin brothers Sts Floros and Lauros falls on 18 August. Curiously, the same pair of saints is represented, in medallions once again, in the outer narthex (see III. 7). This repetition probably means that the coordination between those who commissioned the art and the artists was not entirely effective, that the artists who worked on the chapel differed from those who worked on the naos and the narthexes, or that this pair of saints were accorded particular prominence – perhaps because they were connected with those interred in the nearest arcosolium in the chapel. Repetition of depicted persons in Christian art is not exceptional, at least in the later Balkan tradition.

In the bottom register of the south wall, a representation of a saint survives with the following inscription:

– ὁ Ἅγι(ος) Θεόδωρος ὁ Τ[ή]ρω[ν] (Τίρων) – St Theodore Teron (17 February);

On the south wall, the images of the following martyrs also survive:

– ὁ Ἅγι(ος) Θεόδωρος (ὁ Στρατηλάτης) – St Theodore Stratelates (8 February);
– [ὁ Ἅγιος] Μερκούριος – St Merkourios (25 November);
– ὁ Ἅγι(ος) Προ[κόπι]ος – St Prokopios (8 July);
– ὁ Ἅγι(ος) Σάββας ὁ Στρα[τηλάτης] – St Sabbas Stratelates (18 April).

On the north wall, near the entrance to the chapel, next to Arcosolium A, associated by researchers with Theodore Metochites, is depicted:

– ὁ Ἅγι(ος) Δα(βὶ)δ ὁ ἐν Θεσσαλονίκῃ – St David of Thessaloniki (26 June). The abbreviation for the name of David here is identical to that in Cod. Dujčev Gr 177, where f. 13 r reads as follows: κστ΄ (μηνὶ ἰουνίω) τοῦ ἁγίου δα(βὶ)δ θεσ(σ)αλονίκῃ ζήτ' ὀκτ(ωβρίω) κα΄) – *26 June of St David of Thessaloniki, see 21 October.*

The choice of these saints is not related to the calendar, but rather to intercession for those laid to rest in the chapel.

It is worth mentioning that St Theodore Stratelates is represented missing his right shoe, that is, this is the *monosandalos* type, rare in Christian iconography.[143] In the tradition of the Old Testament, taking off one's shoe (sandal) is described in Ruth 4:7 as 'the manner in former time in Israel concerning redeeming and concerning changing, for to confirm all things; a man plucked off his shoe, and gave it to his neighbour: and this was a testimony'.

It is possible that St Theodore Stratelates was Metochites' patron, with his representation as μονοσάνδαλος testifying to a deal with Tornikes. Another possible explanation for the missing sandal might be found in Exodus 3:5: . . . *put off thy shoes from off thy feet, for the place whereon thou standest is holy ground.* And indeed, the site of a tombstone should not be trodden upon, especially in footwear. *Losing one's shoe from off one's feet* before entering a house of prayer is also found also in Deuteronomy 25:9, Joshua 5:15. The depiction of St Theodore Stratelates should probably be connected with the representation of *Moses and the Burning Bush*; a viewer entering the chapel would see Moses removing his shoe in the scene to the right above Tomb D, and St Theodore Stratelates missing his right shoe on the left, next to Tomb D.[144]

Burial Recesses (Arcosolia) (A–D in Figure 7)

As has been indicated earlier, the question of the burials in the Chora, particularly in *parekklesion*, is one of crucial importance in piecing together the church's role and history. In what follows, I will give an account of what is known of these monuments, but also advance my own theory as to the set of dynastic connections they represent.

There are four burial recesses in the *parekklesion*, A–D. Only two of them (C and D) provide an indication of the types of the burials and their decoration. Both, however, are in poor condition, having been restored as far back as the Byzantine period. Tomb E, in the outer narthex, also retains some decoration. These three monuments will be described and discussed first, before moving on to the wider picture.

A sarcophagus in the chapel's apse was also found by L. Majewski during excavations on 10 November 1958. This was considered by Ousterhout a post-fourteenth-century addition.[145] This underfloor tomb (2.10 m in length) covered with two marble slabs and then with the floor tiles is oriented east-west and

[143] Some researchers associate this type with the Greek tale of Jason. This hero stood before King Pelias holding a spear, as St Theodore Stratelates is represented at the *parekklesion* in the Chora, wearing panther skin and only one sandal. Then Jason was sent with the Argonauts to steal the Golden Fleece from Kolchis.

[144] Moutafov, *Богородица*, pp. 119–120.

[145] Ousterhout, *Architecture*, p. 60.

placed at the exact centre of the bema. The hole in the middle of the slabs was broken in Ottoman times and there is no skeletal evidence available.[146]

No systematic excavations have been carried out in the burial places, though the Ottoman floor tiles in the *parekklesion* have been removed. There is no certainty whether these spaces were intended for primary burials or for the transfer of disinterred bones, for single or for multiple burials or even for symbolic ones (the painted portraits above arcosolia may suggest the latter).[147] Some of the mortal remains of those interred here may have been translated to other places, to judge by the scenes in the iconographic programme relating to moving the Ark of the Coventant: *Κιβωτός* ('Ark' in Greek) also means 'coffin'. All the graves in the Chora had been disturbed at some point before Turkish floor tiles were placed. Only for Tomb A in the *parekklesion* do we have a single piece of evidence, written by Ernest Hawkins, dating to 3 September 1959, who reports to Paul Underwood in a letter that 'going down to a depth of nearly 1.5 m skull and bones [were found]' without mentioning even the sex (male or female), age, dating of the remains, or their *in situ* condition.[148]

Tomb D – The Tornikes Monument (see Figure 17)

In some ways, Tomb D is the most straightforward to deal with. Here, nobly garbed images of a Grand Constable[149] Michael Tornikes[150] and his wife are depicted flanking a representation of the Virgin and Child.[151] Originally executed in mosaic, the depiction of the deceased couple was repaired in fresco.[152]

Depicted on soffits to either side are a monk and a nun, whose inscriptions read: + ὁ αὐτὸς μοναχός| Μακάριος – *the same person, the monk Makarios*, and + ἡ αὐτὴ μο[ναχῆ] Εὐγενία – *the same person, the nun Eugenia.*[153] It would appear that this is a case of 'double portraits', in which the dead are depicted twice, once in secular clothes, and once in monastic vestments.[154] The surviving decoration of this tomb may indicate that members of the Constantinopolitan aristocracy who then took monastic vows were also interred in the other tombs in the Chora.

Two of the tomb façades preserve traces of polychrome pigments; Tornikes' burial recess retains gilding on its carved surfaces, which are brilliant examples of Late Byzantine tomb sculpture.[155]

This tomb is the only arcosolium in the Chora to preserve a carved funerary epigram *in situ*, attributed to the well-known Byzantine poet Manuel Philes

---

[146] Gerstel, 'The Chora Parekklesion', pp. 134–135. [147] Ibidem, p. 134. [148] Ibidem.
[149] Honorary Byzantine court title ('count of the stable'), later adopted by the Normans.
[150] *PLP*, no. 29132. [151] Ousterhout, 'Temporal', p. 73. [152] Ibidem.
[153] Underwood, *The Kariye*, I, pp. 269–270, 276–280; for the name of his wife *PLP*, no. 29132.
[154] Ousterhout, 'Temporal', pp. 73–74. [155] Brooks, 'Sculpture', p. 101.

Figure 17 Tomb D of Michael Tornikes and his wife, fourteenth century, funeral chapel (*parekklesion*) of the Chora. Photo: Author

(died c. 1345).[156] A. Rhoby's Greek edition and English translation of the epitaph can be found in Appendix 2.[157]

It is unclear exactly who these people were. In the epigram, this Tornikes is described as being of royal lineage. Given that his portrait indicates that his monastic name was Makarios, Orthodox tradition would suggest that his birth name also began with 'M'. In the same period, for example, Andronikos II took the monastic name Antony when he abdicated.[158] Tornikes' wife's birth name, likewise, would have begun with 'E', since her monastic name was Eugenia.

There is only one widely accepted assumption about this Tornikes, which is that his first name was Michael. He has been identified by some as Michael Asan Palaiologos Komnenos,[159] son of King Ivan Asan III of Bulgaria, and his wife as Eirene, sister of Andronikos II Palaiologos.[160] This Michael was one of Andronikos II Palaiologos' inner circle, and a close associate of Theodore Metochites. The opponents of this identification suggest that this Michael

[156] *PLP*, no. 29817; Ševčenko, 'Theodore Metochites', p. 21, ref. 14.
[157] Rhoby, *Byzantinische Epigramme*, pp. 643–650.
[158] *Byzantine Monastic Foundation*, 1254–1255, no. 9.
[159] Nicol, *The Byzantine Family*, p. 152; *PLP*, no. 1514.
[160] Schmalzbauer, 'Die Tornikioi', p. 131; Kubina, 'Manuel Philes', p. 186f.

died in Serbian territory.[161] Whatever the case, this Michael Asan vanishes from the records in 1328.[162]

Another possibility that has been suggested is that the Michael Tornikes of the Chora was Michael Asan Komnenos Tornikes Palaiologos,[163] grandson of the aforementioned King Ivan Asan III and son of Constantine Asan (Isaak Asan's brother). This possibility is often dismissed because he died young, before 1355, as governor of Lesbos. He is, however, known to have been buried in Constantinople.[164] It is noteworthy that the lunette of the Tornikes monument at the Chora includes scenes depicting the translation of a coffin. In his case, Tornikes was evidently his mother's surname.[165] Moreover, Michael Asan Komnenos Tornikes Palaiologos married another Eirene, Eirene Komnene Kantakouzene Palaiologina Asanina,[166] making the monastic name Eugenia very possible.

Given that, as will be seen, there was a strong connection between the poet Manuel Philes and the Asan family, the epitaph on the tomb certainly supports the idea of a connection between Tomb D and either a son or grandson of Ivan Asan III, member of the Asan family. This identification would also fit with other suggestions about the dynastic connections (Asan-Raoul-Dermokaites) represented at the Chora.

Tomb E (outer narthex)

Only fragments of decoration survive in the case of Tomb E in the outer narthex. These show monograms of king Ivan (Ioannes) Asan III Mytzes[167] and of the Palaiologoi. On the basis of this, it has been supposed that this was the tomb of Eirene Asanina Raoulina Palaiologina, daughter of Michael VIII and wife of Ivan Asan III, who died, according to Underwood, in 1332.[168] This identification is debatable.

One of the characters represented in the mid-fourteenth-century painting above Tomb E is identified as a nun named Athanasia.[169]

The poets St John of Damascus and St Kosmas the Melodist are also depicted again around Tomb E, and the inscriptions on the scrolls they are holding have been published.[170] In other words, the hymnographers from the dome of the chapel should not be associated with Metochites alone.

[161] Schmalzbauer, 'Die Tornikioi', p. 131. [162] Bozhilov, *Фамилията Асеневци*, p. 262.
[163] Fatouros and Krisher, *Johannes Kanatkouzenos*, p. 226. [164] Rhoby, *Byzantinische*, p. 647.
[165] Bozhilov, *Фамилията Асеневци*, p. 290. [166] Ibidem, II № 24, pp. 316–317.
[167] Ivan III Mytzes Asan who died in 1302 was made emperor of Bulgaria in 1279 by Michael VIII Palaiologos. See *PLP*, no. 1501.
[168] Underwood, *The Kariye*, IV, pp. 284–286; 3; pl. 450–451. This hypothetical identification and dating of her tomb influenced the entry in *PLP*, no 24142 and Ousterhout, 'Emblems', p. 93. In fact the written sources say very little about this Eirene.
[169] See Bacci, 'Tomb G', p. 114. [170] Underwood, *The Kariye*, III, pp. 544–545.

Figure 18 Tomb C, fourteenth century, funeral chapel (*parekklesion*) of the Chora. Photo: Author

Tomb C (see Figure 18)

The same combination of monograms of the Asans and the Palaiologoi as found in Tomb E is also present in Tomb C, the south-east tomb in the chapel.[171]

Tomb C is similar to the Tornikes monument; it is painted in fresco, but its occupants have not been identified. Four figures were painted in the lunette, three of which are in expensive clothes, whereas a nun depicted on the right may be the second portrait of the adjacent female image.[172]

Tomb A (see Figure 19)

It is Tomb A that, in my opinion, holds the key to understanding the burials at the Chora.

As has been said, a question that has preoccupied scholars of the Chora is where Theodore Metochites planned to be buried. Traditionally, most scholars have agreed that tomb A was Metochites' tomb: it is the largest in the chapel, with the best setting, and this interpretation is considered to be reinforced by the iconographical programme.[173] Moreover, it would have placed him opposite

[171] In his legend, it is Tomb D opposite the Tomb B. See Mango and Ertug, *Chora*, p. 243, plan on p. 33.

[172] Ousterhout, 'Temporal', p. 74.

[173] Ibidem, pp. 63–76; for the archaeological evidence, see Ousterhout, *The Architecture*, p. 199.

Figure 19 Tomb A, fourteenth century, funeral chapel (*parekklesion*) of the Chora, Photo: Author

Tornikes, his friend and ally. This theory assumes that the occupant of Tomb D was the son of Ivan Asan III, not the grandson.

An exception to this interpretation is Sharon Gerstel's suggestion that Metochites was buried beneath the floor of the apse of the *parekklesion*, where a Late Byzantine sarcophagus was found;[174] in support of this, she cites an *ekphrasis* from Cyprus and an archaeological dig in Italy,[175] and does not think that the iconography around Tomb A suggests the presence of a more prominent occupant.[176] Gerstel's suggestion has been described by Ousterhout as a position that would have been 'both unusual and quite possibly heretical'.[177]

As will be seen, I also hold that Tomb A was not intended for Metochites, but I cannot agree with the idea that he planned to lay himself to rest beneath the slabs of the apse of the *parekklesion*. He did indeed have the power to break all the rules, choosing the most visible place for his entombment, but an Orthodox Christian would hardly assent to the idea of his resting place being trodden, even for celebrating the Eucharist. After all, the altar of the *parekklesion* was also intended for performing services. Relics of saints were usually placed under the Holy Table to maintain the palaeo-Christian tradition of celebrating the

[174] Gerstel, 'The Chora Parekklesion', pp. 129–145. Semoglou thinks the Despotes Demetrios Palaiologos may have been buried in the ground in front of the apse of the *parekklesion*; see Semoglou, 'The Anastasis', p. 93.

[175] Ibidem, p. 135. [176] Ibidem, p. 136. [177] Ousterhout, *Finding a Place*, p. 65, ref. 68.

Eucharist upon the relics of a martyr, but it is unlikely that Metochites would have thought it appropriate to be buried there.

Moreover, if he intended to be buried in Tomb A opposite Tornikes, son of Ivan Asen III, it remains a mystery why Metochites, himself a poet, would have missed the chance to compose an epitaph for Tornikes and leave his own poetic mark on his own monastery. This Michael Tornikes is believed to have died four years before Metochites, when such a gesture would have been a distinct possibility. However, it was Philes whom the descendants of the couple buried in Tomb D commissioned to perpetuate the memory of their relatives.

This connection with Manuel Philes starts to point in a different direction. Philes had contact with at least three members of the Asan family, namely the brothers Isaak, Andronikos, and Michael, as shown recently by Krystina Kubina.[178] This relationship with the Asan family lasted from at least 1316 until the 1330s, making the Byzantium-based Asans regular clients and sponsors of Philes.

Most importantly for interpreting the Chora, Philes was commissioned by Isaak Asan to compose two epitaphs for his mother Eirene (Irene) Asanina Komnene Palaiologina,[179] where she is called ἡ ... βασιλὶς Βουλγάρων Ἀσανίνα – or *Queen of the Bulgarians, of the Asen dynasty.*[180] Eirene, daughter of Michael VIII Palaiologos, was an enormously significant figure in the history of the Asan family, but also in wider Byzantine history, since it was she who married Ivan Asan, founding the Asan dynasty. Her numerous children went on to build family connections across the higher echelons of Byzantine society.

The question is still open, however, as to the identity of the church where Eirene Asanina, for whom the epitaphs were written, and other members of the Asan family were to be buried. Kubina, analysing the text Isaak Asan commissioned from Philes, suggests that their burial place was a similar setting to the *parekklesion* of the Pammakaristos. This was a chapel with acrosolia, patronised by another family, the Glabas, who commissioned decoration of the church and, notably, also epitaphs by Philes.[181] Especially interesting is a section in Eirene Asanina's epitaph, which reads as follows (for the Greek text, see Appendix 3):

> *(. . . Her fleeting body is asleep), but it is prepared for the marvelous resurrection 85 For another earthly birth may happen, when the mouth of the trumpet shall sound, bringing together the limbs in a second creation. But the one, who is lying buried and painted with shadows [here], here looks to the only*

[178] Kubina, 'Manuel Philes', p. 197. [179] *PLP*, no. 21359.
[180] Kubina, 'Manuel Philes', p. 183. [181] Ibidem, pp. 193–194.

> *blameless one [the Virgin Mary] 90, for in life, too, she had her as a protector and guardian of her thrice fortunate children and her good hopes for the future.* (Translated by K. Kubina)[182]

Kubina argues that the epitaph must have been carved for Eirene's grave and transferred to a painted arcosolium (ἡ κειμένη δὲ καὶ σκαιγραφουμένη – *placed and painted by using the effects of light and shade*); this is also suggested by the use of the pronouns ἐνθάδε (here) and τάδε (so). The verb σκιάζω (shade) is also used in a text of the same century, dealing with the technique of icon painting, but in the sense of 'contour drawing *using the effects of light and shade*'.[183] Here σκιαγραφία means drawing, painting as opposed to mosaic techniques such as those used in the Chora *naos* and narthexes.

I believe that what Philes describes here would fit with an identification of Eirene Asanina's burial place as Tomb A; it seems to describe precisely a burial at the Chora, remodelled on more than one occasion,[184] with a painting of the figure of the deceased (the Greek verb indicates a drawing not a painting), and in a setting that would reflect the iconographic programme of the Chora *parekklesion*. The text was highly likely inscribed in pigment on the wall of Tomb A or on a slab beneath the arch, which has been later removed.

Numerous parallels between the Philes epigram and the location of Tomb A would support this interpretation. Tomb A, in accordance with the description in the epitaph, would have placed Eirene Asanina, *painted with shadows* expecting her *marvellous resurrection* (the *Anastasis* in the altar conch), *when the mouth of the trumpet shall sound* (the *Last Judgement* in the adjacent dome), protected by the Virgin Mary (Mary with angels in the dome immediately above Tomb A) *with her thrice fortunate children* and grandchildren.[185] Philes' idiosyncratic ekphrasis also describes Eve from the *Resurrection* in v. 18, as well as Eirene's father, Michael VIII – 25 *The famous Michael, the crown wearer (which the same to say), her sweet father, the Palaeologan, an Angel also with regard to his nature . . .* ;[186] this can be connected with the figure of the archangel Michael (IV.3, see Figure 15), and possibly the angel with the soul of a dead man in the north-west pendentive of the domical vault (IV.11). Philes even describes a tablet with stars, sun, and moon symbolising the universe, held by an angel, reminiscent of the

[182] Ibidem, pp. 183–185.

[183] Parpulov et al., 'A Byzantine Text', pp. 201–216. This text on Byzantine painting technique from the fourteenth century also suggests a form of existence of such manuals during the Late Byzantine period, which were used later for the sources of Dionysius like Priest Daniel's opus and the so-called First Jerusalem Codex, published by A. Papadopoulos-Kerameus.

[184] Ibidem, p. 194. [185] Kubina, 'Manuel Philes', pp. 184–185. [186] Ibidem, p. 184.

scene of the *Last Judgment* in the Chora *parekklesion*: *Sun and Earth and last thunders*![187]

My contention, then, is that Tomb A was the tomb of Eirene Komnene Asanina Palaiologina, and that she was the first to be interred in the funeral chapel, c. 1321, certainly after 1317. By that time, her involvement in the conflict between Andronikos II and the Catalan company in 1306, when she sided with her son-in-law Roger de Flor, would have no doubt been forgotten, and as a Byzantine by blood and a queen of the Bulgarians by marriage, it would have been fitting for her to be interred at a monastery of high standing located between the Blachernai and the Pantokrator.

This identification, moreover, has consequences for interpreting the other tombs in the *parekklesion*: Manuel Philes' epigram speaks of Eirene's children, 'thrice fortunate', echoing the description of Tornikes as ὁ τρισαριστεὺς. Accordingly, it seems probably that the other burial recesses were intended for Eirene's children.

On this basis, I consider it likely that Tomb C was the burial place of Eirene's son, Isaak Asan, who commissioned her epitaph and might well have been a donor of the Chora. He married Theodora Archantloun, daughter of the Maria Palaiologina[188] represented in the Chora *Deesis*. My opinion is that Isaak Asan with both his wives was represented after 1351 in the lunette of Tomb C: Theodora (left) and the unknown second wife (to the right of the male figure), as well as his daughter from his second marriage, Eirene Philanthropena (on the far right). Theodora died c. 1351, bearing no children.[189]

Of the two potential candidates for Tomb C, the most famous arcosolium, I believe that it was the burial place of the grandson of Ivan Asan III, Michael Tornikes, and his wife Eirene, but not in 1328, for it is highly unlikely that after the abdication of Andronikos II Palaiologos both his follower and the wife of the latter could have succeeded in taking monastic vows and dying in the same year. This must have happened between 1328 and 1340, during Manuel Philes' lifetime, when the atelier that painted the Chora was still functioning.

Only Tomb B gives no indication of its burial; its decoration is now lost. Eirene Asanina's epitaph, however, suggests that one of her sons was entombed there. It is unlikely that it was Andronikos Asan,[190] because he married the daughter of the *protostrator*[191] Michael Doukas Glabas Tarchaneiotes[192] and therefore was probably interred in the Glabas funeral chapel in the Pammakaristos.[193] My suggestion is that it was, rather, another son, Constantine Asan.[194] Constantine, together with his brother Andronikos, the Grand Logothete Theodore Metochites,

[187] Ibidem, verse 72, p. 185. [188] Bozhilov, *Фамилията Асеневци*, p. 276. [189] Ibidem.
[190] *PLP*, no. 1488. [191] Byzantine court official, originating as the imperial stable master.
[192] *PLP*, no. 27504. [193] Bozhilov, *Фамилията Асеневци*, p. 285. [194] *PLP*, no. 1503.

the Protovestiarios[195] Andronikos Kantakouzenos, and the Grand Papias[196] Constantine Tornikes, signed the treaty of 1324 between Byzantium and the Venetian Republic.[197] Constantine's name precedes even that of Metochites: ... καὶ τοῦ περιποθήτου ἀνεψιοῦ τῆς βασιλείας μου κυρίου Κωνσταντίνου Παλαιολόγου τοῦ Ἀσάνη ... 'by my dear nephew' (Constantine was Andronikos II Palaiologos' nephew) *Constantine Palaiologos Asan*.[198] In 1328, Constantine led the troops of Andronikos II in the battle against the pretender to the throne, Andronikos III, in Eastern Thrace. After the defeat, Constantine Asan was taken into captivity, and until 1341 nothing was known about him.[199] His wife's name is also unknown, but given that Michael Komnenos Tornikes Asan Palaiologos (Tomb C) was his son, she was presumably a member of the Armenian Tornikoi.[200]

Thus, the burials of the Chora attest to a genealogy of mortals – privileged burials, bound together by ties of kinship – parallel to the genealogies of Christ and the Most Holy Mother of God in the iconographic programme of the inner narthex of the Church. This horizontal and non-divine line of descent begins with Maria Palaiologina depicted in the *Deesis* (II.4) to go to her sister and her sister's sons and grandchild. The burials go further, entombing probably more members of the Palaiologoi, Tornikoi, and Asans, to come to that of Eirene Asanina Raoulina Palaiologina, yet another daughter of Michael VIII, as it was believed until now.[201]

The presence of Eirene Asanina and her descendants in the Chora *parekklesion* thus lend Metochites' monastery continued prestige through their imperial blood, providing a patronage probably very necessary for financial reasons. His money probably ran out at a certain stage of the decoration. This is the only explanation I can provide for the fact that the chapel was decorated with murals rather than with mosaics, as the former are easier, cheaper, and can be executed more quickly by fewer painters. Metochites' role in setting out the structure of the Church and, above all, of its decoration must have remained significant, but the story then leads on to later donors. That, I believe, is why the space to the right of Jesus in the *Donor Portrait*, although it remains empty, diagonally leads the eye to the representation of the nun Melania, as a key link in that chain.

An additional observation is that there are indications that the north-west of the church may have been intended as the burial place of further aristocratic

[195] High Byzantine court position, originally reserved for eunuchs.

[196] Usually eunuch official in the Eastern Roman Empire court, responsible for the palaces in Constantinople.

[197] Bozhilov, *Фамилията Асеневци*, p. 288.

[198] Guilland, 'Le Grand connétable', p. 225, etc.

[199] Ioannes Cantantacuzenos, *Ex Imperatoris*, I, p. 415.

[200] Such an assumption has already been made by Bozhilov, *Фамилията Асеневци*, p. 290.

[201] Underwood, *The Kariye*, IV, pp. 284–286; 3; pl. 450–451; Ousterhout, 'Emblems', p. 93.

figures. This is suggested by the positioning of the tomb of the Despotes Demetrios Palaiologos, son of Andronikos II, under the depiction of genealogy of Christ in the inner narthex, to the left of the *Donor Portrait*, and in opposition to the depiction of Isaak Komnenos in the *Deesis*, which may indicate that other members of the Palaiologoi, who were not of Mongolian, Bulgarian, or Armenian lineage, were to be interred in this area of the church.

Whether or not my interpretation of the burials of the Chora is accurate, it is in any case beyond doubt that the evidence attests the presence of Palaiologoi, Asans, Raouls, Dermokaites (the existence of monograms of the Dermokaites family is clear), and Tornikoi in the burial recesses. This indicates the significance of the Chora as an alternative for privileged burials of a lower rank than those of the imperial *heroon* at the fourteenth-century Pantokrator. The presence of descendants of the Bulgarian royal dynasty also shows that the Byzantine οἰκουμένη was flexible and open to communication with the aristocracy of the neighbouring Orthodox nations, irrespective of the endless battles waged against them. This family line of the Byzantium-based Asans was evidently regarded as an imperial dynasty and this is why its members received similar treatment to the Palaiologoi. An additional piece of evidence dating from 1390s shows that the *hegoumenos* (abbot) of the Chora monastery Kornelios was in contact with a woman named Anna Asanina Palaiologina, who Melvani considers may have been a relative of the families represented in the Chora arcosolia; an additional proof that these nobles were closely connected with the monastic community almost a century after Metochites passed away.[202]

Diakonikon

In Theodore Metochites' time, the *diakonikon* was separated by a wall from the bema of the main church and linked to the new side chapel; thus, the *diakonikon* of the *naos* became the *prothesis*[203] of the *parekklesion*. Underwood supposed that it might have been used as a baptistery, because a small round container was found under the apsidal area of the *diakonikon*.[204] Such a combination of baptistery and funeral chapel is, of course, unacceptable. The 'baptismal font' under the apse was apparently a form of θαλασσίδιον (small thalassa – bathing pool) or a χωνευτήριον (piscina). What can be said is that we have here a vessel or a container, whatever its liturgical or pragmatic function.

In my opinion, the *diakonikon*, as part of the funeral chapel, is the sole separate chamber that could have housed the mortal remains of Theodore Metochites.

202 Melvani, 'The Last Century', pp. 1238–1239.
203 The area where the Liturgy of Preparation takes place.
204 Underwood, *The Kariye*, IV, p. 23.

Apparent similarities have been observed earlier between the Pantokrator and the Chora in terms of their planning and functioning. The *heroon* at the Pantokrator, where members of the Komnenian and the Palaiologan dynasties were entombed, is a separate domed chamber between two churches, and, very much like that at the Chora, was dedicated to the Archangel Michael. Both monuments were apparently also modelled on the Holy Sepulchre in Jerusalem.

The Chora *diakonikon*, viewed eastwards from outside, still looks like a small separate church. In Metochites' time, this chamber was deliberately separated from the naos, so that it could no longer function as *diakonikon*. I think that Metochites most likely planned to be buried in this chamber. It is incorporated into the funeral chapel, but independent, being an aedicule (small shrine) like that in Jerusalem. It is also a brightly lit area, which would have served to accentuate its significance: apart from three east windows, it has also windows in the drum of the dome. Its entrance is right beneath Christ's outstretched hand from the Resurrection scene. Thus, a cycle of the iconographic programme is formed: Metochites, presenting Christ with a model of the Chora in the *Donor Portrait*, achieves in exchange eternal life from the Saviour, applying the ancient Roman principle of reciprocity *do ut des*. The piscina in the *diakonikon* possibly alludes to Theodore's assumed monastic name Theoleptos or 'containing God'. It may well mark the spot where the donor's body was to be placed in a sarcophagus on the floor; besides, wine could, following common practice, be poured into this vessel at memorial services, as probably described in the Chora Typikon, modelled on the typika of the Pantokrator and the Kosmosoteira.

There are only a few parallels for this in the history of Orthodoxy; however, some examples can be cited. For example, the anonymous *Vita Constantini* (c. 715–1005) relates that Empress Helena founded the church in Jerusalem on the site of the Last Supper, where on the left side of the *diakonikon* a tomb of King David was set up.[205] King David was the patron of poets such as Metochites, and the presence of Jerusalem is keenly felt in the iconographic programme of the fourteenth-century Chora. There are also later occurrences of burials in *diakonikons*. In the sixteenth century, Tsar Ivan IV the Terrible (1553–1584) and his son Ivan Ivanovich, as well as tsar Feodor (1557–1598), were buried in the *diakonikon* of the Cathedral of the Archangel Michael, in the Kremlin, in purpose-built sarcophagi. Ivan IV was also garbed in the vestments of a *schemamonk*.[206]

Taking into consideration a range of factors – the proposed interments at the Chora, described here, Metochites' egocentricity, the liberties he took with

[205] An Arabic source of the ninth century contains the same information. See Pringle, *The Churches*, p. 262.

[206] Voronov, *Спасо-Преображенский*, p. 41.

manipulating the painting and architectural canons, and his lack of relationship to those buried in Tombs B, C, and D – I believe that he planned to lay himself to rest in the *diakonikon*, to be the first to be raised up by Christ's right hand at the future resurrection of the dead. This is why no clear evidence has been found for his presence in the decoration of the chapel, whether through a monogram, portrait, or inscription.

Calvary Crosses are discernible on the extant fragments of the decoration in the *diakonikon* with letters forming the *Christogram* IC XC| NI KA = Ἰ(ησοῦ)ς Χ(ριστὸ)ς νικά – *Jesus Christ conquers* (the soffit of the arch, north wall),[207] laden with soteriological significance and performing apotropaic functions as the flank bordering spaces. A weathered fresco of five of Christ's disciples is still discernible in the dome of the *diakonikon*.[208] This group of Apostles may be compared to the prophets waiting to be raised from the dead to the right of Christ in the apsidal conch of the chapel.

The traces of unimposing decoration in the *diakonikon/prothesis* once again suggest that this was the decoration of a chamber where a dead man was to be interred. Until now these murals were believed to have been painted in the twelfth century, but in my opinion (published in 2020), the use of crosses bearing letter marks is a clear sign of a trend that emerged in the late thirteenth century, involving a certain group of monuments of Palaiologan art. The earliest known case of this is the Church of the Virgin Peribleptos in Ohrid (1295), from where it later spread to other monuments such as the Church of St Nicholas the Orphanos, Thessaloniki and the *katholikon* of the Graćanica monastery, Kosovo (1321) (associated with the atelier of Michael Astrapas and Eutychios), and then further to monuments painted by other artists, such as the fourteenth-century funeral chapel of the Holy Archangels, Monastery of Bachkovo, the Church of St John the Theologian, Zemen, and even reaching as far as Curtea de Argeş. Thus, this idiosyncratic trend of painting crosses bearing cryptograms covered a vast area between Ohrid, Bachkovo, Graćanica, Staro Nagoričane, Thessaloniki, Constantinople, and Curtea de Argeş, and in the fifteenth century, besides the Balkans, spread on a large scale to Cyprus.[209]

The decoration of the Chora *diakonikon* is certainly not of the twelfth century,[210] but it is difficult to say whether or not it was its final version, that

[207] Underwood, *The Kariye*, III, p. 529. [208] Ibidem, p. 528.

[209] Moutafov, 'Криптограмите', pp. 139–149, esp. p. 147.

[210] An important point here is that decorations from the twelfth century have not survived in the other parts of the Chora either. In 2023, Athanasios Semoglou also suggested that the renovation and painting of the Chora *diakonikon* should be dated to the fourteenth century. In his interpretation, it may have been transformed into a space intended to house the tomb of Prince Manuel Palaiologos. See Semoglou, 'The Anastasis', p. 94.

is, intended to house the burial of the main donor. It is usually descendants who undertake the ultimate decoration of a grave as, for instance, Isaak Asan did with the tomb of his mother.

It cannot be known, however, whether Metochites was indeed eventually buried, if these were indeed his plans, in the *diakonikon*. After being ousted from office and impoverished, he came back to the Chora as a simple monk, in inevitably modest circumstances. However, as a potential burial place for him, Tomb A, opposite the Tornikes monument, which has been previously suggested, is too unimposing, providing neither privacy nor uniqueness, while the *diakonikon* is a small church modelled on the *heroon* at the Pantokrator and, above all, on the *kouvouklion* in the Holy Sepulchre in Jerusalem. Ultimately, however, the question of the precise place of Metochites' interment can only be determined, if at all, by archaeological excavations.

The Testimony of Inscriptions and Artistic Technique

In 2016, Nikoleta Troupkou received a doctorate from the Aristotle University of Thessaloniki for her thesis *The Greek Script in Wall Mosaics of the Late Byzantine Period*,[211] which has made a significant contribution to understanding not just the inscriptions themselves but also the connections between the writers, the artists, and the fourteenth-century building work on the Chora.

Using the tools of epigraphy and palaeography, Troupkou argued convincingly that seven writers were responsible for the inscriptions that accompany the Chora mosaics and frescoes.[212]

Of these writers, the first was responsible for most of the inscriptions on the theologically most significant scenes, such as the mosaics of Christ Pantokrator (the 'Land of the Living') and Mary the 'Container of the Uncontainable' in the outer narthex, the *Donor Portrait*, the surviving *naos* mosaics, the *Deesis*, St Peter, the Healing Miracles, the *Life of the Virgin* in the inner narthex, about seventeen scenes in the outer narthex, and the portraits of Michael Tornikes and his wife in the *parekklesion*. Troupkou believes that this anonymous writer was also a mosaicist, assuming that he was the leading master painter at the Chora, because some of the characteristics of his writing have been adopted by other writers in the workshop. The latter, in turn, are deemed by Troupkou to be disciples of the leading master painter/writer.[213]

The second anonymous writer also executed, amongst other inscriptions, a significant number of those in the inner narthex (the martyrs, the Virgin

[211] Troupkou, *Η ελληνική γραφή*. [212] Ibidem, vol. 1, p. 175. [213] Ibidem.

Blachernitissa), as well as the inscription on the tomb of Demetrius Palaiologos. This writer is also believed to have been both a scribe and a painter.

The further five writers are minimally represented in the surviving iconographic programme. Two of the rarest scenes, *Joseph's Dream* with *The Journey to Bethlehem* and the *Enrolment for Taxation* in the outer narthex, are attributed to the sixth writer (see Figure 13). Troupkou argues that the first and sixth writers worked on both the mosaics in the *naos* and the two narthexes *and* the mural paintings in the chapel. Most of the inscriptions on the latter were made by the first writer or leading master, while those in the centre of the *Last Judgment* composition, Melchizedek, and the four hymnographers in the pendentives were executed by the sixth one.[214]

I agree entirely with these observations, because my own research also shows that an atelier of seven to ten men worked here, two of whom were particularly important. The leading master sketched the compositions and depicted the most delicate parts of a human figure, such as the face and hands, while journeymen executed backgrounds, garments, and nimbi, mixed the pigments, and took the materials up to the scaffolding. Commissions like those at the Chora were particularly taxing and undoubtedly an established atelier of eminent and highly erudite masters was commissioned to execute it. In other words, this would not have been their first commission, and the members of the wider team were replaced over the five long years, at least at the level of the journeymen and the writers. The two main painters whose work can be identified by the two styles in the executed mosaics preferred to work with the best-performing disciples, who did the inscriptions. It was only the two of them, together with a single disciple each, who worked in the *parekklesion*, as the wall painting technique did not require a large team, and they, apparently, did not favour one. My observations regarding the mural painting of later periods suggest that one master with one disciple could cover three square metres a day, using painting techniques,[215] that is, four men worked for about half a year at the Chora. It would have taken twice as many men and twice as much time to execute the mosaics, as mosaic-making techniques are far more sophisticated.

According to Troupkou, this atelier was probably based in Constantinople and most active between 1290 and 1340, with the master craftsmen being replaced over the years. Members of this atelier also worked on the first paint layer at the Pammakaristos (c. 1310), and after 1315 were commissioned to decorate the Church of the Holy Apostles in Thessaloniki. This atelier was most active in Thessaloniki between 1328 and 1334.[216] Initially, the painters were commissioned by Nephon I (Patriarch of Constantinople 1310–1314).

[214] Ibidem, p. 176. [215] Moutafov, 'Texts', p. 249. [216] Zapheires, *Θεσσαλονίκης*, p. 176.

Nephon I is an interesting contemporary of Theodore Metochites. He enjoyed a lavish lifestyle, fancied thoroughbred horses and expensive clothes, was a gourmet and patron of the arts, took the liberty of constructing new buildings using the revenues from convents, and was ousted for the sin of simony.[217] During his stint in power, however, in Constantinople Nephon, I founded only the small Monastery of the Theotokos Peribleptos, a far cry from the glory and popularity of the Chora. Owing to his background (born in Veroia) and time possibly spent in Thessaloniki and on Mt Athos, his major project was instead the Church of the Holy Apostles in Thessaloniki.[218]

The artists' work in Thessaloniki began with mosaics, but after Nephon resigned as Patriarch in 1314, and above all after his death in 1333, with funding becoming scarcer, the decoration was completed using mural techniques under the supervision of *Hegoumenos* Paul. The same happened at the Chora: painting replaced mosaics due to a shortage of funds.

The main writer attached to the atelier returned to the Chora after the death of Michael Tornikes in 1328 to decorate his tomb in the funerary chapel. The atelier also participated in the second stage of the decoration of the Pammakaristos under the supervision of Michael Tarchneiotes' widow. According to Troupkou's inferences, the seventh writer was commissioned in 1340 to decorate the tomb of Demetrios Palaiologos in the Chora.[219] In other words, palaeographic analysis proves that masters from the same atelier came back to the Chora until at least 1340, which again suggests Metochites was much less important in Chora than most scholars have suggested.

It is especially interesting to note here that masters such as Astrapas and Eutychios, who came from the second largest city in the empire – Thessaloniki – recorded their names in the same century, while the gifted and erudite Constantinopolitan artists from the atelier based in the capital, who worked at the Chora and the Pammakaristos, have remained anonymous. An explanation for this might be a clash of authority between Theodore Metochites and the artists, which would be in keeping with what is known of Metochites' character. The evidence suggests that in some ways, the painters themselves were no less educated than their patron, judging by the inscriptions they left and the scenes they executed, which, as far as is known, have no precursors in Byzantine tradition. The commissioning and theological instructions alone cannot explain the final results, which required both talent and wide experience; and in the case of these artists, their previous

[217] Agoritsas, 'Ὁ Οἰκουμενικός', p. 262. [218] Charalampides, 'Η προσωπικότητα', p. 283, 285.
[219] Troupkou, *Η ελληνική γραφή*, pp. 176–177.

commissions brought a great deal of experience, which increased their self-confidence.

Besides painting, these artists possibly also undertook the construction work carried out in Metochites' day; it is perfectly feasible that this could have been done by a team of ten or so members over a period of five years, as suggested by Young.[220] The palaeographic characteristics of the epitaph on the Tornikes tomb, written by the authors of the mosaics and the murals, show that they were well versed in stonemasonry. This assumption, moreover, would explain the close relationship between the architecture and iconography of the monument; as Ousterhout observes, '[T]he iconographic program and the unusual spatial setting were planned together.'[221]

Evaluation

The mosaics of the Chora reflect the brilliance of Constantinopolitan art. Most scenes unfold within a complex architectural scenery in the background, largely reminiscent of the Hellenistic artistic heritage. The saints are depicted in uncommon positions – almost as if hovering – and from different angles; they were probably inspired by several sources, such as Byzantine manuscripts[222] and working sketches.[223] The general effect is largely that of lyricism and smoothness, compared to thirteenth-century Byzantine frescoes, and this is especially evident in the scenes from Christ's childhood.[224] What is especially impressive is the new perception of artistic space, with the human forms and the landscape presenting a harmonic, ethereal whole, despite the fact that there are several axes, even vertical ones, applied, especially in the multi-person scenes. This is evident in the scene of the *Annunciation*, where the edifices in the background face each other, creating a triangle that provides the frame for the main scene.

From an artistic point of view, the wall paintings of the Chora do not rely on rendering any limitation through the contour but on toning up the contrast between the coloured surfaces. The colours are more saturated, brighter, and livelier – often even unnatural – and they remind us more of enamel artwork; they differ completely from the ascetic style of eleventh- and twelfth-century painters.

[220] Young, 'Relations', pp. 269–278. [221] Ousterhout, *Finding a Place*, p. 41.

[222] For example, the codices Par. gr. 510, Par. gr. 115, Laur. Plut. VI, 23, etc.

[223] Millet, *Recherches*; Underwood, *The Kariye*, pics 17, 24–28, 48, 57, 58 in Demus' paper; figs. 2, 319, 21, 24–27, 29, 32, 34, 35, 43, 46, 50, 52, 55, 60, 63 in Lafontaine-Dosogne's paper; figs. 18, 23–25 in Underwood's paper.

[224] Schmit, *Мозаика*, p. 159.

The technique of the frescoes is very similar to the mosaics of the narthex; the compositions are free-handed and forceful; the shapes are light with smooth folds in the clothing and similar colour motifs. Both completely differ from the austere vertical arrangement of frescoes and icons of the twelfth century. The heads of the people are somewhat stereotypical, while the facial characteristics are soft and thin. Despite the similarities, from an artistic point of view, the mosaics are on a higher level than the frescoes, indicating the existence of work designs prior to placing the tesserae.[225] The mosaics also show a wider colour range and better use of colour, and have been better preserved. The frescoes, on the other hand, create a sense of melancholy, show a somewhat persistent repetition of techniques, and have a more austere effect. A few decades after these frescoes were created, their strict and severe technique would dominate Byzantine art.[226]

The processes of rediscovery of classical ideals, of humanist ideas, of humanist ideas, of nature and colour, were similar in Western Europe and Byzantium – parallel at times, independent of each other at others. Thirteenth-century Western Europe was still dominated by the Gothic style that came to life in the north of France as early as the second half of the twelfth century to spread across the continent in opposition to the Romanesque style, which was not so focused on human suffering.[227] The Late Byzantine period in Balkan arts ended in the first half of the fifteenth century with the emergence of a style combining classicism and abrupt movements and hugely impactful colours. The last shining examples of such a high art are associated with Mystras, Greece.[228] It was only the Ottoman conquest that put an end to the development of a genuine Renaissance in the Balkans, which would have been, in all likelihood, equal in brilliance to the Italian one.[229]

Within these developments, the artists who decorated the fourteenth-century Chora were mirror images of some of the Italian greats, such as Cimabue (1240–1302) and, above all, Giotto (1266–1337), who laid the groundwork for Masaccio (1401–1428); however, they developed their art independently of Western Gothic imagery, and subject to the constraints of the commissions and Orthodox convention.

The Chora, being one of those monuments of Byzantine art where the human and the divine meet and wrestle, attracts wide-ranging interest from people across generations and cultures. However, despite the significant amounts of information available about and by its donors, as well as the good condition, to date, of the decoration, nevertheless there are few clues about the artists themselves, and this

[225] Lazarev, *История*, p. 161. [226] Underwood, 'Palaeologan Narrative', pp. 6–9.
[227] *The Oxford Companion to Art*, p. 491.
[228] Panselenou, *Η βυζαντινή*, pp. 240–247. [229] Demus, 'The Style', pp. 136–139.

intricate monument continues to tantalise and bewilder those who seek to unravel its mysteries. Whatever truth one may discover about the Chora, however objective one tries to be, can be by no means conclusive or exhaustive.

The Post-Byzantine Years

Being in the immediate vicinity of Constantinople's Adrianople Gate, the Chora was among the first buildings to fall to the Ottomans in 1453. During the final siege, the sacred palladium of the city, the wonderworking icon of the Virgin, said to have been painted by St Luke, was kept at the Chora, providing spiritual defence against the enemy. On 29 May, having entered the city by the Adrianople Gate, Ottoman soldiers found their way to the Chora and were ordered to break the venerable icon into pieces, looting its silver revetment and symbolically annihilating the protective powers of the icon.[230]

Around 1512, when the Chora was repurposed as a mosque, known as the Kariye Camii, the mosaics and the murals were covered with a thin layer of mortar, to protect Muslim sensitivities about depictions of the human form. In 1568, the German traveller Stefan Gerlach left a description of the church, now mosque, noting that the mosaics and the murals were still slightly visible through the plaster.[231]

After the Chora was converted to a mosque, a church dedicated to the Virgin *ton Ouranon* ('of the heavens', Salmatomruk Panagia Kilisesi) was built in the same district of the city, very close to the complex.[232] This epithet corresponds to that associated with the Blachernitissa representation of Mary, *Platytera ton Ouranon* (Wider than the Heavens), and because of its location it seems clear that the church was a successor to the Byzantine one. There is clear evidence for the existence of this church in the seventeenth and eighteenth centuries,[233] and it was completely renovated in 1834.[234]

On the western façade of the Salmatomruk Panagia Kilisesi, there is an interesting stone relief with an unusual pyramidal architectural composition, which includes three churches and a double arched gate; on the top is a smiling sun (see Figure 20 and compare with Figure 10).[235] The central building is the biggest, and is highly stylised, but it has five arched entrances just like the blind arches on the western façade of the Chora. This stone slab does not correspond

[230] Ousterhout, *The Art*, p. 15. [231] Ibidem, p. 16. [232] Janin, *La geographie*, p. 223.

[233] Papadopoulos-Kerameus, 'Ναοὶ', pp. 118–145.

[234] 'ὁ ναός οὗτος τῆς Παναγνοῦ Παρθένου ἠγέρθη ἤδη ἐκ θεμελίων ἐκ νέου . . . 1834 Ἀπριλίου 1[H]' – *This church of the All-pure Virgin was re-erected from scratch . . . on 1 April 1834* as it is published in Karaca, *İstanbul'da Tanzimat*, p. 255. The author calls the church Salmatobruk Panagia.

[235] Karaca, *İstanbul'da Tanzimat*, p. 256.

Figure 20 Triple church structure on the west façade of the Orthodox Church Panagia ton Ouranon, renovated in 1834. Photo credit: Zafer Karaca

to the other two on the same wall, which have crosses in relief and are of regular quadrangular shape. This makes me believe that it is older – probably from the sixteenth/seventeenth-century structure. The most important detail here is that the composition is unlike the profile of post-Byzantine churches in the Balkans. That gives me reason to presume that it is an image of another and older church, which could be the Chora, and that the smaller extensions of it are the later churches dedicated to Virgin in the same *chora/mahalle*[236] – Salmatomruk Panagia and Panagia Tekfur Saray[237] – as a syncretism[238] of the local cult and Greek nostalgia for the glorious past of Constantinople.

After the Second World War, the Chora/Kariye ceased to be a functioning mosque. In 1958, it was opened as a museum administered by the Ministry of Culture and Tourism, religiously neutral ground in a secular state as conceived

[236] The Kariye mosque was surrounded by its own mahalle ('district' or 'administrative unit'), as it probably also had been in the Byzantine period. Süleyman, *Converted*, p. 76.

[237] The existence of this church was mentioned in 1652, 1669, and 1800. The contemporary presentation of the building is a result of renovations carried out in 1837. Karaca, *İstanbul'da Tanzimat*, p. 265.

[238] On such syncretism, but between Christian buildings and Muslim functions, and especially on the transformation of the trapeza of the Chora to a türbe, see Oustehout, *The Architecture*, pp. 86–87 and fig. 147; Ousterhout, 'Contextualizing', p. 243.

by Kemal Atatürk. As a result of this, visitors and scholars from around the world interested in familiarising themselves with Constantinople's past could visit this brilliant example of Palaiologan art, photograph and record the fragmentary surviving decoration, study, and learn.

In the summer of 2020, however, Turkey's President Recep Tayyip Erdogan changed the jurisdiction over the Chora; the monument is now administered by a religious institution, the Directorate General of Foundations. In recent years, the Directorate General has gained control of other Byzantine monuments and reopened them to Muslim prayer.

At the time of writing, the Chora remains closed, with the explanation that this is connected with ongoing preservation work. Furniture required for converting the monument to a mosque has been installed in the interior. A system for covering the mosaics and frescoes has also been installed and tested.

Successive Byzantine, Ottoman, and Turkish governments have protected the Chora against the ravages of time. One can only hope that future Turkish governments will honour the heritage, preserve the monument, and make it fully accessible to all (including diakonikon).

Appendices

Appendix 1

Dedicatory Poem of Maria Palaiologina

Cod. Dujčev Gr 177, 244 r-245 v; see Figures 5 and 6

+ Στίχοι ἱκετήριοι πρὸς τὴν Δέσποιναν καὶ Παρθένον καὶ Θεομήτορα τὴν Χωρινὴν ὡς ἐκ προσώπου τῆς εὐσεβεστάτης δεσποίνης κυρᾶς Μαρίας Κομνηνῆς τῆς Παλαιολογίνης

+ Ἔδει μὲν ἴσως τῇ παναχράντῳ Κόρῃ,
τῇ παρθένῳ καὶ σῶμα καὶ τὴν καρδίαν,
τῇ τῶν Χερουβὶμ καὶ Σεραφὶμ κυρίᾳ,
τῇ τῶν ἁγίων αγιωτέρᾳ νόων
5 ἀξίαν ἀντίχαριν ἀποτιννύειν
ὑπὲρ τοσαύτης εὐμενοῦς εὐσπλαχνίας
καὶ τῆς ἀφράστου πρὸς Χριστὸν παρρησίας,
τὸν Ὑιὸν αὐτῆς καὶ Θεὸν καὶ Δεσπότην,
ὑπὲρ ἀγάπης τῆς βροτῶν σωτηρίας
10 ἣν καθ' ἑκάστην δεικνύει Χριστωνύμοις,
οἷα μόνη σώζουσα καὶ λυτρουμένη
τούτους ἁπάσης τῶν ἐναντίων βλάβης.
Ἔδει προσάξαι πλὴν μετ' εὐνοίας ὅσης
βασιλικὸν τὸ δῶρον ὡς Βασιλίδι
15 ἀνθ' ὧν παρ' αὐτῆς ἀπέλαυον χαρίτων,
ἀνθ' ὧν μυρίων ἐκλυτροῦμαι κινδύνων
τῇ συμμαχίᾳ καὶ κραταιᾷ δυνάμει
τῆς πανσθενουργοῦ καὶ πανυμνήτου Κόρης
ἀλλα τίς ἰσχύσειν οὕτως ἀξίως
20 τὸ κοσμολαμπὲς δεξιώσασθα φάος,
τὴν τῶν ἁπάντων ὑπερηρμένην νόων;
Ἐφ' ᾧπερ ὡς ἔχοιμοι πλὴν μετὰ δέους,
μετὰ δακρύων καὶ καθαρᾶς καρδίας,
μεθ' ὧνπερ ηὐπόρησα πέπλων χρυσέων
25 καὶ τὴν ἱερὰν τήνδε βίβλον προσφέρω
τῷ σεβασμίῳ τῆς παναχράντου δόμῳ
(Χώραν καλεῖν εἴωθεν ἅπας τὸν δόμον)
αὐτῆς συνάρσει τῆσδ' ἐπὶ γῆς τῆς ξένης
ταύτην τυχοῦσα σὺν ἀκοσμίᾳ τόσῃ,
30 εἰ καὶ λίθων ἦν ἔνδοθεν σὺν μαργάροις
ὥσπερ διαυγὴς στιλπνότης ἢ χρυσίον
τὰς ἡλιακὰς ἀκτῖνας ὑπερβάλλον

οἱ Κυριακοὶ χρύσεοι θεῖοι λόγοι,
δι' ὧν πᾶσα γέγηθε πιστῶν καρδία,
35 δι' ὧν κόσμος σέσωστο Σατὰν τῆς πλάνης,
πλὴν ἀλλὰ κοσμήσασα ταύτην σὴν πόθῳ,
καθώσπερ εἶχον ἐκ χρυσοῦ σὺν αργύρῳ,
ἐκ χρυσοϋφοῦς κοκκινοχρόου πέπλου,
ἐκ καρδιακοῦ τοῦ πόθου Σοὶ προσφέρω,
40 Δέσποινα Μῆτερ τοῦ Θεανθρώπου Λόγου,
Μαρία λάτρις οἰκέτις Σοῦ γνησία,
Παλαιολόγων ἐκ γένους κατηγμένη,
ἡ τῆς Ἑῴας βασιλὶς τῆς ἁπάσης.
Ἀλλ' εὐμενῶς μοι, παμβασιλίς, προσέχου
45 ἃ Σοὶ προσάγω σὺν ζεούσῃ καρδίᾳ,
εἰ καὶ τέως πέφυκεν οὐ κατ' αξίαν,
καὶ πρὸς μονὰς σκήνου με τὰς οὐρανίους,
πρὸς τὴν ἀγήρω τῆς Ἐδὲμ κατοικίαν.

Verses of supplication to the Despoina (empress) Virgin and Mother of God of the Chora as if spoken in person by the very pious empress lady Maria Komnene Paliologina

It was equally appropriate (for me) to repay
A worthy return of a favor to the all-pure Maiden,
Virgin both in body and heart,
To the mistress of the Cherubim and Seraphim,
To the one more holy than the holy angels,
In return for much favorable mercy
And for her unspeakable freedom of speech before Christ,
Her son, both God and Lord,
In return for her love of the salvation of human beings,
Which she shows every day to Christians,
Since she alone saves and redeems
Them from every harm of their enemies.
It was appropriate (for me) to bring, yet with great affection,
A gift of royal character, as if to an empress,
For recompensation of the goods I enjoyed from her,
For recompensation of the innumerable dangers I am saved from
By the alliance and mighty strength
Of the all-powerful and ever-praised Maiden.
But who would be able to so worthily
Honour the world-illuminating light,
The one elevated above all angels?
Given that, as best I can, yet with fear,
With tears and pure heart,
Along with the golden veils that I richly possessed,
I also offer this sacred book

to the venerable house of the all-pure (Maiden).
(Everyone is accustomed to call the house Chora).
With her assistance on this alien (i.e. mortal) earth
found it with utterly no ornamentation,
Although the interior was of (precious) stones with pearls,
Just like sparkling glitter of goldness
Which surpasses the rays of the sun,
(Namely) the Lord's golden divine words,
Through which every heart of the faithful rejoices,
Through which the world has been saved from the error of Satan.
But yet, having had this (book) decorated out of desire,
As best I could, with gold along with silver,
With a red-coloured veil woven with gold,
(O) mistress mother of the God-Man Word
I offer (it) from my heart's desire to you,
Maria, your genuine maid-servant,
Descended from the family of the Palaiologoi,
the empress of the whole Orient.
But with favour toward me, Empress of all, pay attention
To what I bring you with burning heart,
Although at present it is not of equal value.
And make me come to dwell in the heavenly mansions,
In the never-ageing house of Eden.[1]

[1] Edition and translation by N. Teteriatnikov; also found in Krăstev, 'A Poem', pp. 71–77.

Appendix 2

Epitaph of Michael Tornikes by Manuel Philes; see Figure 17

Ὅσους ἂν ἀθροίζοι τις ἐνθάδε κρότους
νεκροὺς ὁ ταφεὶς ἐξελέγξει Τ ορνίκης[2]|
ὁ τρισαριστεὺς ἢ κονοσταῦλος μέγας
ὥσπερ μίμους, βέλτιστε, πιθήκους λέων·|
5 ὃς βασιλικῶν ἀποτεχθεὶς αἱμάτων
παρέσχεν αὐτοῖς προσφυῆ καὶ τὸν τρόπον·
ποῖον γὰρ οὐκ ἦν ἀρετῆς εἶδος φέρων,|
ὡς ὁ πρέπων ἕκαστον ἐζήτει χρόνος;
Βουληφόρος δ' οὖν καὶ πρὸ τῆς ἡλικίας
10 καὶ δημαγωγὸς καὶ κριτὴς ἦν ἀνχίνους|
καὶ πρὸς μὲν ἐχθροὺς τακτικῆν ἔπνει φλόγα
κεραυνὸς ὢν ἄφυκτος αὐτοῖς ἀθρόοις·||
τῇ δὲ στρατιᾷ π(α)τρικῶς ἐπεστάτει
φρουρῶν τὰ κοινά, μὴ κλαπῇ τὸ συμφέρον·|
15 κήδους δὲ τυχὼν εὐγενοῦς καὶ κοσμίου
καὶ βασιλικὸν προσλαβὼν αὖθις γένος|
καὶ λαμπρὸν ὑπόδειγμα παρεὶς τὸν βίον
κεῖται μοναστὴς εὐτελὴς ἐν ὀστέοις·|
ἥλιε καὶ γῆ καὶ τελευταῖοι κρότοι,
20 πενθεῖ δὲ μικροῦ πᾶν τὸ Ῥωμαίων γένος,|
ὅσονπερ αὐτὸν ἀγνοοῦν οὐ τυγχάνει·
ἀλλ' ὦ μόνε ζῶν καὶ μεθιστῶν τὰς φύσεις,|
εἴ πού τι καὶ πέπραχεν αὐτῷ μὴ πρέπον,
λύσιν παρασχὼν τὴν Ἐδὲμ κλῆρον δίδου.

However many applauses one may collect upon this earth,
When they are all dead, Tornikes, a man of myriad
Or Grand Constable, who lies buried here, [victories,
Will put them to shame as, good friend, a lion shames
5 *He who was by birth of royal blood, [mimicking apes.*
Present also a manner of life conformed to that [descent.
For what form of virtue did he not possess
Such as the fitting occasion demanded each?
Therefore he was a councillor before the usual age,
10 *and a popular leader and an acute judge,*
And upon enemies he breathed a strategic flame,
And was an irresistible thunderbolt upon their serried
He presided over the army like a father, [ranks.
Guarding the commonweal lest any advantage to it should be

[2] In the original, each line of the poem ends in three vertical dots.

15 *contracting a highly-born and seemly marriage [stolen.*
And securing thus again royal affinity, [connection,
And leaving his life as a splendid example,
He lies a poor monk among bones!
O sun, O earth, O final applauses!
20 *Well-nigh the whole Roman race laments him,*
As much of it as is not ignorant of him.
But O only living One and transformer of natures,
If perchance he did aught that was not fitting for him,
Granting him pardon, give him Eden as his inheritance.[3]

[3] As edited and translated in Underwood, *The Kariye*, I, pp. 276–277.

Appendix 3

Section of the Epitaph of Eirene Asanina Komnene Palaiologina by Manuel Philes

. . . πρὸς τὴν ξένην ἔγερσιν ηὐτρεπισμένον.
85 ἄλλος γὰρ ἂν γένοιτο καὶ γῆθεν τόκος,
εἴπερ τὸ τῆς σάλπιγγος ἠχήσοι στόμα
προς δευτέραν τὰ κῶλα συλλέγον πλάσιν.
ἡ κειμένη δὲ καὶ σκαιγραφουμένη
90 πρὸς τὴν μόνην ἄμεμπτον ἐνθάδε βλέπει,
κἀν τὸ βίῳ γὰρ εἶχεν αὐτὴν προστάτιν
καὶ τῶν τόκων φύλακα τρισλοβίων
καὶ τῶν ἀγαθῶν εἰς τὸ μέλλον ελπίδων.
For the English translation see p. 58.

Bibliography

Primary Sources

Byzantine Monastic Foundation Documents, ed. J. P. Thomas and A. Hero (Washington, DC: Dumbarton Oaks Series, 2000).

Cantantacuzenos, I., *Ex Imperatoris Historiarum Libri*, ed. L. Schopen (Bonn: University of Bonn, 1828), vol. I.

Codex Apocryphus Novi Testamenti, ed. I. C. Thilo (London: Wentworth Press, 2019).

Dionysius of Phourna (Fourna), *Ἑρμηνεία τῆς ζωγραφικῆς τέχνης*, ed. A. Papadopoulos-Kerameus (St Petersbourg: Russian Holy Synod, 1909).

Enc. Greg. Pal. 133 Tsames = Gregoriou tou Palama, *Συγγράματα*, I-III (Thessaloniki: Kyromanos, 1962–1970).

Georgios Pachymeres, *De Michele et Andronico Paleologis libri tredecim*, rec. I. Bekkerus (Bonnae, 1835).

Ioannes Cantatacuzenos, *Ex Imperatoris Historiarum Libri*, ed. L. Schopen Vol. I. (Bonn: University of Bonn, 1828).

Nikephoros Gregoras, *Historia Byzantina*, ed. L. Schopen, 2 Vols. (Bonn: University of Bonn, 1829).

Literature

Agoritsas D., 'Ὁ Οἰκουμενικός Πατριάρχης Νίφων Α΄ (1310–1314)', *Ἐπιτηρίς Ἑταιρείας Βυζαντινῶν Σπουδῶν*, Vol. 53 (2007–2009), 232–269.

Anderson J., 'The Seraglio Octateuch and the Kokkinobaphos Master', *Dumbarton Oaks Papers 36* (1982), 83–114.

Angelov D., 'Asia and Europe Commonly Called East and West: Constantinople and Geographical Imagination in Byzantium', in *Imperial Geographies in Byzantine and Ottoman Space*, S. Bazzaz, Y. Batsaki and D. Angelov (eds.) (Washington, DC: Center for Hellenic Studies, 2013), 43–68.

Bacci M., 'Tomb G at the Chora and the Illusion of Presence' in *Biography of a Landmark: The Chora Monastery/ Kariye Camii in Constantinople/ Istanbul from Late Antiquity to the 21st Century*, Manuela Studer-Karlen (ed.) (Leiden: Brill 2023), 100–134.

Bakirtzis Ch., *Βυζαντινά τσουκαλολάγηνα* (Athens: Minsitry of Culture, 1989).

Beck H. G., *Theodoros Metochites: Die Krise des byzantinischen Weltbildes im 14. Jahrhundert* (München: C. H. Beck, 1952).

Berger A., 'Imperial and Ecclesiastical Processions in Constantinople' in *Byzantine Constantinople: Monuments, Topography and Everyday Life*, N. Necipoğlu (ed.) (Leiden: Brill, 2001), 73–87.

Boeck E., *The Bronze Horseman of Justinian in Constantinople: The Cross-cultural Biography of a Mediterranean Monument* (Cambridge: Cambridge University Press, 2021).

Bozhilov I., *Фамилията Асеневци (1186–1460): Генеалогия и просопография* (Sofia: Bulgarian Academy of Sciences, 1985).

Brooks S., 'Sculpture and the Late Byzantine Tomb' in *Byzantium: Faith and Power (1261–1557)*, Helen C. Evans (ed.) (New York: Metropolitan Museum of Art, 2003).

Bydén B., *Theodore Metochites' Stoicheiosis astronomike and the study of natural philosophy and mathematics in early Palaiologan Byzantium*, 2nd rev. ed. Acta Universitatis Gothoburgensis. Studia Graeca and Latina Gothoburgenisa 66 (Göteborg: University of Göteborg, 2003).

Charalampides K., 'Η προσωπικότητα τοῦ Πατριάρχη Νήφωνα Α΄ ὡς χορηγοῦ τοῦ ναοῦ τῶν Ἁγίων Ἀποστόλων Θεσσαλονίκης', *Βυζαντινά*, 19 (1998), 283–287.

Demus O., *Byzantine Mosaic Decoration: Aspects of Monumental Art in Byzantium* (New York: Caratzas Brothers, 1976).

'The Style of the Kariye Djami and Its Place in the Development of the Palaeologan Art' in *The Kariye Djami*, P. A. Underwood (ed.) (Princeton University Press, 1975), Vol. 4, 107–160.

Der Nersessian S., 'Program and Iconography of the Frescoes of the Parekklesion' in *Late Classical and Medieval Studies in Honor of Albert Mathias Friend,* Jr K. Weitzmann, S. der Nersessian, G. H. Jr. Forsyth, E. H. Kantorowicz and Mommsen, T. E. (eds.) (Princeton: Princeton University, 1975), 303–350.

Džurova A., 'La décoration des manuscrits grecs et slaves (IXe -XIe siècles)', *Scripta*, 1, 2008, 45–59.

Fatouros G. and T. Krisher, *Johannes Kanatkouzenos: Geschichte: Erster Teil*, Buch I (Stuttgart: Bibliotek der griechischen Literatur 17, 1982).

Gedeon M. I., Θεόδωρος ὁ ἀρχαιότερος κτίτωρ τῆς μονῆς τῆς Χώρας. Ὁ ἓν Κωνσταντινούπολει *Ελληνικός φιλολογικός σύλλογος*, τόμ. XXIV-XXVI, 19–23.

Gennadios of Helioupolis (Heliopoleos), 'Ὁ Πατριάρχης Φιλόθεος Κωνσταντινουπόλεως περὶ τῆς ὀνομασίας τῆς μονῆς τῆς Χώρας', *Ὀρθοδοξία*, 22 (Constantinople: Ecumenical Patriarchate, 1947), p. 278.

Gerstel S., 'The Chora Parekklesion, the Hope for a Peaceful Afterlife, and Monastic Devotional Practices' in *Kariye Camii Reconsidered*, H. Klein, R. Ousterhout and B. Pitarakis (ed.) (Istanbul: İstanbul Araştırmaları Enstitüsü, 2011), 129–145.

Gioles N., *Βυζαντινή ναοδομία (600–1204)* (Athens: Kardamitsa, 1992).

Grabar, A. 'The artistic climate in Byzantium during the Palaelogan period' in *The Kariye Djami. Studies in the Art of Kariye Djami and Its Intellectual Background*, Underwood, P. A. (ed.) (Princeton: Princeton University Press, 1975), 3–16.

Guilland R., 'Le Grand connétable', *Recherches sur les Institutions Byzantines*, t. 1 (Berlin: Akademie-Verlag, 1967), 469–477.

Hetherington P., *The Painter's Manual of Dinoysius of Fourna* (London: Oakwood, 1981).

Hunger H., 'Theodoros Metochites als Vorlaufer des Humanismus in Byzanz', *Byzantinische Zeitschrift* 45 (1952), 4–19.

Jacoby D., 'The Urban Evolution of Latin Constantinople (1204–1261)', in *Byzantine Constantinople: Monuments, Topography and Everyday Life*, N. Necipoğlu (ed.) (Leiden: Brill, 2001), 277–297.

Janin R., *La geographie ecclesiastique de l'empire Byzantine*, I 3 (Paris: Institut français d'études byzantines, 1969).

Jolivet-Lévy, C., 'La peinture à Constantinople au XIIIe siècle. Contacts et échanges avec l'Occident' in Orient et occident méditerranéens au XIIIe siècle: les programmes picturaux, Caillet, J.-P., Caillet and F. Joubert (eds.) (Paris: Picard, 2012), 21–40.

Jordan R. (trans.), 'Typikon of Pantokrator Monastery' in *Byzantine Monastic Foundation Documents*, J. P. Thomas and A. Hero (ed.) (Washington, DC: Dumbarton Oaks Series, 2000).

Kalokyres K., *Ἡ Θεοτόκος εἰς τὴν εἰκονογραφίαν ἀνατολῆς καὶ δύσεως* (Thessaloniki: Patriarchal Patristic Research Foundation, 1972).

Karaca Z., *İstanbul'da Tanzimat öncesi Rum Ortodoks Kilisereli* (Istanbul: Yapı Kredi Yayınları, 2008).

Kondakov N. P., *Мозаики мечети Кахрие-Джамиси – μονή τῆς Χώρας – в Константинополе* (Odessa: G. Oulrich Printing House, 1881).

Kotzageorgis Ph. P., 'Two Vakfiyes of Mara Branković', *Hilandarski zbornik* 11 (2004), 307–322.

Krăstev G., 'A Poem by Maria Comnene Palaeologina from Manuscropt No 177 of the Ivan Dujčev Centre for Slavo-Byzantine Studies', *Byzantinoslavica* LVIII 1 (1997), 71–77.

Krautheimer R., *Early Christian and Byzantine Architecture* (Baltimore: Penguin Books, 1965).

Kubina K., 'Manuel Philes and the Asan Family: Two Inedited Poems and Their Context in Philes' oeuvre (including editio princeps)', *JÖB* 63 (2013), 177–198.

Kuniholm P. I. and C. L. Striker, 'Dendrochronological Investigations in the Aegean and Neighboring Regions, 1983–1986', *JFA* 14, no. 1 (1987), 385–398.

Lazarev V. N., *История византийской живописи* (Moscow: Iskusstvo, 1986).

Lafontaine-Dosogne J., 'Iconography of the Cycle of the Life of the Virgin' in *The Kariye Djami: Studies in the Art of Kariye Djami and Its Intellectual Background*, P. A. Underwood (ed.) (Princeton: Princeton University, 1975), 161–194.

'Iconography of the Cycle of the Infancy of Christ' in *The Kariye Djami: Studies in the Art of Kariye Djami and Its Intellectual Background*, P. A. Underwood (ed.) (Princeton: Princeton University, 1975), 195–242.

Lidov A., 'Icon as Chora: Spatial Aspects of Iconicity in Byzantium and Russia' in *L'icone dans la pensée et dans l'art*, K. Mitalaité et A. Vasiliu (ed.) (Leiden: Brepols, 2017), 427–439.

Magdalino P., 'Theodore Metochites, the Chora, and Constantinople' in *The Kariye Camii Reconsidered*, H. Klein, R. Ousterhout and B. Pittarakis (eds.) (Istanbul: İstanbul Araştırmaları Enstitüsü, 2011), 169–187.

Mango C., *Byzantinische Architektur* (Stuttgart: Belser Verlag, 1975).

Mango C. and A. Ertug, *Chora: Scroll of Heaven* (Istanbul: Ertug & Kocabiyik, 2000).

Melvani N., 'The Last Century of the Chora Monastery: A New Look at the Tomb Monuments', *Byzantinische Zeitschrift* 2021, 114(3), 1219–1240.

Millet G., *Recherches sur l'iconographie de l'Évangile aux XIVe, XVe et XVIe siècles, d'après les monuments de Mistra, de la Macédoine et du Mont-Athos* (Paris: Fontemoing et CIE, 1914).

Moutafov E., 'Μονή Χώρας (Καριγιέ Τζαμί)/ Chora monastery (Kariye Camii)' in Εγκυκλοπαίδεια της βυζαντινής Κωνσταντινούπολης (Αθήνα 2009), 10 pp.; Greek version: http://constantinople.ehw.gr/forms/fLemma.aspx?lemmaid=10900&contlang=57 Greek version: http://constantinople.ehw.gr/Forms/fLemma.aspx?lemmaid=11767&contlang=58.

'Криптограмите и билингвизмът на Палеологовото изкуство', *Patrimonium* 3(2010), 139–149.

'On How to "Read" the Chora Monastery', *Medioevo Greco* 16 (2016), 199–212.

'Texts, Inscriptions, and Images in the Church of St Nicholas, Monastery of Bachkovo' in *Texts – Inscriptions – Images, Art Readings – Old Art Module*, E. Moutafov and J. Erdeljan (eds.), Vol. I (2016), Institute of Art Studies, 247–260.

Богородица Вместилище на Невместимото. Човешки измерения на Палеологовото изкуство в Константинопол (Sofia: Professor Marin Drinov Publishing House of Bulgarian Academy of Sciences, 2020).

Митрополитският храм „Св. Стефан" в Несебър и неговият художествен кръг: културен контекст, интертекстуалност и интервизуалност (Sofia: Bulgarian Academy of Sciences, 2022).

Müller-Wiener W., *Bildlexikon Zur Topographie Istanbuls: Byzantion, Konstantinupolis, Istanbul Bis Zum Beginn D. 17 Jh.* (Tübingen: Wasmuth, 1977).

Nelson R., 'The Chora and the Great Church: Intervisuality in Fourteenth-Century Constantinople', *Byzantine and Modern Greek Studies* 23 (1999), 67–101.

'Taxation with Representation: Visual Narrative and the Political Field of the Kariye Camii', *Art History* 22 (1999), 56–82.

Nicol D. M., *The Byzantine Family of Kantakouzenos (Cantacusenus), ca. 1100–1460* (Washington, DC: Dumbarton Oaks Series XI, 1968).

Oates D., 'A Summary Report on the Excavations of the Byzantine Institute in the Kariye Djami: 1957 and 1958', *Dumbarton Oaks Papers* 14 (1960), 223–231.

Ousterhout R. G., *The Architecture of the Kariye Camii in Istanbul* (Washington, DC: Dumbarton Oaks Research Library and Collection, 1987).

'The Virgin of the Chora: An Image and Its Contexts' in *The Sacred Image: East and West*, R. G. Ousterhout and L. Brubaker (ed.) (Urbana: Illinois University Press, 1995), 91–109.

'Temporal Structuring in the Chora Parekklesion', *Gesta*, Vol. 34, No 1 (1995), 63–76.

'Contextualizing the Later Churches of Constantinople: Suggested Methodologies and a Few Examples', *Dumbarton Oaks Papers* 40 (Washington, DC, 2000), 231–249.

'Architecture, Art and Komnenian Ideology in the Pantokrator Monastery' in *Byzantine Constantinople, Monuments, Topography and Everyday Life*, N. Necipoğlu (ed.) (Leiden Köln: Brill, 2001), 133–150.

The Art of the Kariye Camii (Istanbul: Scala, 2002).

'Reading Difficult Buildings: The Lessons of the Kariye Camii' in *The Kariye Camii Reconsidered* H. Klein, R. Ousterhout, and B. Pitarakis (ed.) (Istanbul: Istanbul Araştırmaları Enstitüsü, 2011), 87–99.

'Emblems of Power in Palaiologan Constantinople' in *The Byzantine Court: Source of Power and Culture*, A. Odekan, N. Necipoğlu and E. Akyurek (eds.) (Istanbul: Koc University Press, 2013), 89–94.

Finding a Place in History: The Chora Monastery and Its Patrons (Nicosia: Leventis Foundation, 2017).

Oxford History of Byzantium, C. Mango (ed.) (Oxford: Oxford University Press 2002).

Panselenou N., *Η βυζαντινή ζωγραφική. Η βυζαντινή κοινωνία και οι εικόνες της* (Athens: Kastaniotes, 2002).

'Introduction' in *Biography of a Landmark. The Chora Monastery/Kariye Camii in Constantinople/Istanbul from Late Antiquity to the 21st Century*, Manuela Studer-Karlen (ed.) (Leiden: Brill 2023), 1–14.

Papadopoulos-Kerameus A., 'Ναοὶ τῆς Κωνσταντινουπόλεως κατὰ τὸ 1583 καὶ 1604', *Ἑλληνικὸς φιλολογικὸς σύλλογος* XXVIII, 118–145.

Papageorgiou P. N., 'Αἱ Σέρραι καὶ τὰ προάστεια, τὰ περὶ τὰς Σέρρας καὶ ἡ μονὴ Ἰωάννου τοῦ Προδρόμου', *Byzantinische Zeitschrift* III (1894), 326–327.

Parpulov G. R., I. V. Dolgikh and P. Cowe, 'A Byzantine Text on the Technique of Icon Painting', *Dumbarton Oaks Papers* 64 (2010), 201–216.

Pringle D., *The Churches of the Crusader Kingdom of Jerusalem: A Corpus*. Vol. 3 – The City of Jerusalem (Cambridge: Cambridge University Press, 2007).

Prosopographisches Lexikon der Palaiologenzeit (PLP) 12, ed. Trapp E. (Wien 1992).

Rhoby A., *Byzantinische Epigramme auf Stein nebst Addenda zu den Bänden 1 und 2* (Wien: Austrian Academy of Sciences, 2014).

'Theodoros Metochites' *Byzantios* and Other City *Encomia* of the 13th and 14th Centuries, in Dossiers byzantins, 12 (Paris: Centre d'études byzantines, néo-helleniques et sud-est européennes, École des Hautes Études en Sciences Sociales), 81–99.

Richter J. P., 'Abendlandische Malerei und Plastik im Orient', *Zeitschrift für bildende Kunst* XIII (1878), 194–206.

Ryder E., 'The Despoina of the Mongols and Her Patronage of the Church of the Panagia tou Mougoulion', *Journal of Modern Hellenism* 27 (2009), 71–102.

Semoglou A., 'L'éloquence au service de l'archéologie. Les "enfants aimés" de Theodore Métochite et sa bibliothèque dans le monastère de Chora' in *Towards Rewriting? New Approaches to Byzantine Archaeology and Art (Proceedings of the Symposium on Byzantine Art and Archaeology*, Cracow, 8–10/9/2008, ed. P. L. Grotowski and S. Skrzyniarz) – *Series Byzantina* 8 (2010), 45–65.

'The Anastasis in the Funeral Chapel of Chora Monastery in Constantinople: Meaning and Historical Interpretations' in *Biography of a Landmark. The Chora Monastery/ Kariye Camii in Constantinople/ Istanbul from Late Antiquity to the 21st Century*, Manuela Studer-Karlen (ed.) (Leiden: Brill, 2023), 74–99.

Ševčenko I., 'Theodore Metochites, the Chora, and the Intellectual Trends of His Time' in *The Kariye Djami. Studies in the Art of Kariye Djami and Its*

Intellectual Background, Underwood, P. A. (ed.) (Princeton: Princeton University Press, 1975), 17–92.

Seymer V., W. H. Buckler and G. Buckler, 'The Church of Asinou, Cyprus, and Its Frescoes', *Archeologia*, LXXXIII (1933), 336–340.

Schmalzbauer G., 'Die Tornikioi in der Palaiologenzeit', *JÖB* 18 (1969), 120–135.

Schmit F. I., *Мозаика и фрески в Кахриэ-Джами. I История монастыря Хоры. Архитектура мечети. Мозайки нарфиков* (Constantinople: Russian Imperial Archaeological Mission, 1903).

Smyrlis K., 'Contextualizing Theodore Metochites and his Refoundation of the Chora', *Revue des Études Byzantines* 80 (2022), 69–111.

Studer-Karlen M., 'Walking through the Narthex: The Rite in the Chora' in *Biography of a Landmark: The Chora Monastery/ Kariye Camii in Constantinople/ Istanbul from Late Antiquity to the 21st Century*, Manuela Studer-Karlen (ed.) (Leiden: Brill, 2023), 31–73.

Süleyman K., *Converted Byzantine Churches in Istanbul: Their Transformation into Mosques and masjids* (Istanbul: Ege Yayinlari 2001).

Swift E. H., 'The Latins at Hagia Sophia', in *AJA* 39 (1935), 458–474.

Talbot M.-A., 'The Female Patronage in the Paleologan Era: Icons, Minor Arts and Manuscripts' in *Wiener Jahrbuch für Kunstgeschichte*, L. Theis, M. Mullett, M. Grünbart, G. Fingarova, and M. Savage (eds.) Vol. 60 (2012), 259–274.

'The Restoration of Constantinople under Michael VIII', *Dumbarton Oaks Papers* 47 (1995), 243–261.

'Theoleptos' in *The Oxford Dictionary of Byzantium*, A. Kazhdan (ed.) (Oxford: Oxford University, 1991), 2056–2057.

'Building Activity in Constantinople under Andronikos II: The Role of Women Patrons in the Construction and Restoration of Monasteries', in *Byzantine Constantinople: Monuments, Topography and Everyday Life*, N. Necipoglu (ed.) (Leiden: Brill, 2001).

Teteriatnikov N., 'The Dedication of the Chora Monastery in the Time of Andronikos II Palaiologos', *Byzantion* 64 (1996), 188–207.

'The Place of the Nun Melania (the Lady of the Mongols) in the Deesis Program of the Inner Narthex of Chora, Constantinople', *Cahiers Archèologiques* 43 (1995), 165–180.

The Oxford Companion to Art, H. Osborne (ed.) (Oxford: Oxford University Press, 1970).

Το Βυζάντιο ως οικουμένη, ed. Ch. Evangelos (Athens: National Reasearch Foundation, 2001).

Troupkou N., *Η ελληνική γραφή των εντοίχιων ψηφιδοτών της ύστερης βυζαντινής περιόδου* (PhD thesis) (Thessaloniki: Aristotle University of Thessaloniki, 2016).

'Ο τάφος του δεσπότη Δημητρίου στη Μονή της Χώρας και η Παναγία Ζωοδόχος Πηγή', *Βυζαντιακά* 33 (2016), 301–317.

Underwood P. A., 'The Deesis Mosaic in the Kahrie Cami at Istanbul' in *Late Classical and Medieval Studies in Honor of Albert Mathias Friend, Jr.* K. Weitzmann, S. der Nersessian, G. H. Jr. Forsyth, E. H. Kantorowicz T. E. and Mommsen (eds.) (Princeton: Princeton University Press, 1975), 104–121.

'First Preliminary Report on the Restoration of the Frescoes in the Kariye Camii at Istanbul by the Byzantine Institute (1952–1954)', *Dumbarton Oaks Papers* 10 (1956), 253–288.

'Notes on the Work of the Byzantine Institute in Istanbul: 1955–1956', *Dumbarton Oaks Papers* 12 (1958), 267–287.

'Palaeologan Narrative Style and Italian Fresco of the Fifteenth Century in the Karyie Djami' in *Studies in the History of Art dedicated to W. E. Suida on His Eightieth Birthday* (London: Faidon Press, 1959), 6–9.

The Kariye Djami, 4 Vols. (New York: Bollingen Series, 1966).

'Some Problems in Programs and Iconography of Ministry cycles' in *The Kariye Djami: Studies in the Art of Kariye Djami and Its Intellectual Background* (Princeton: Princeton University Press, 1975), 243–301.

Van Millingen A., *Byzantine Churches in Constantinople: Their History and Architecture* (London: Hesperides Press, 1912).

Voronov A. A., *Спасо-Преображенский монастыр на бору – Монастыри Московского Кремля* (Moskow: Publishing House of the St Tihon's Humanitarian University, 2009).

Young S. H., 'Relations between Byzantine Mosaic and Fresco Technique: A Stylistic Analysis', *JÖB* 25 (1976), 269–278.

Zapheires Ch., *Θεσσαλονίκης Ἐγκόλπιον* (Athens: Exantas, 1997).

Acknowledgements

I would like to express my deep gratitude to Professor R. G. Ousterhout (1950–2023), who has devoted the whole of his professional life as an art historian to the monument, for the chance of first visiting the Chora together with him and for helping me year after year with bibliography. I am deeply indebted to Dr Andreas Rhoby for providing publications unavailable to me. I would also like to express my greatest appreciation to Professor Edhem Eldem and Mrs Dafne Bali, who made my work *in situ* in January 2019 easier. I am grateful also to the Series Editor Professor Peter Frankopan, to Dr Judith Ryder who was patient, curious, and very precise in reshaping the initial manuscript I submitted and as a result becoming a very accurate professional reader and model editor for me, to Dr Ida Toth from Oxford University, to Dr Michael Sharp and Julia Ford at Cambridge University Press, to Vibhu Prathima Palamisame from Integra Software Services, and to Professor Elena Boeck for their intellectual generosity in advising me on how to make this text more understandable for the general public, and for the perfect organization of the copy-editing and book design process. This small Element I dedicate to my wife Iliyana, who is my worst critic, but also my ‘uncontainable’ joy.

The History of Constantinople

Peter Frankopan

University of Oxford

Peter Frankopan is Professor of Global History at Oxford University, where he is also Director of the Centre for Byzantine Research and Senior Research Fellow at Worcester College. He specialises in the history of the Eastern Mediterranean from antiquity to the modern day, and is the author of the best-sellers *The Silk Roads: A New History of the World* (2015) and *The New Silk Roads: The Future and Present of the World* (2018).

About the Series

Telling the history of Constantinople through its monuments and people, leading scholars present a rich and unbiased account of this ever-evolving metropolis. From its foundation to the domination of the Ottoman Empire to contemporary Istanbul, numerous aspects of Constantinople's narrative are explored in this unrivalled series.

Cambridge Elements Ξ

The History of Constantinople

Elements in the Series

A full series listing is available at: www.cambridge.org/EHCO

Printed in the United States
by Baker & Taylor Publisher Services